OLD BABYLONIAN TEXTS FROM KISH
CONSERVED IN THE ISTANBUL ARCHAEOLOGICAL MUSEUMS

UNDENA PUBLICATIONS
MALIBU 1986

Bibliotheca Mesopotamica

Primary sources and interpretive analyses for the study of Mesopotamian civilization and its influences from late prehistory to the end of the cuneiform tradition

Editor: Giorgio Buccellati

Assistant Editors: John L. Hayes, Patricia Oliansky

Volume Seventeen

Published Under the Auspices of
IIMAS
The International Institute for Mesopotamian Area Studies

Old Babylonian Texts from Kish Conserved in the Istanbul Archaeological Museums

by Veysel Donbaz
and Norman Yoffee

Undena Publications
Malibu 1986

In this book Donbaz and Yoffee examine legal and administrative texts from Old Babylonian Kish presently conserved in the Istanbul Arkeoloji Müzeleri. The collection and history of Kish during the Old Babylonian period are briefly discussed and the texts are catalogued.

Sixteen texts, all from one month in one year, comprise "a bureau of brick production in Kish during the time of Sinmuballiṭ." Although these bureaucratic memos do not cover the entire range of brick-making activities, they provide information which aids in the reconstruction of a variety of socio-economic institutions at Kish during the reign of king Hammurapi's father. A number of rare terms found in the texts are explicated.

One long contract with its envelope, both only partially preserved, offers an interesting point of departure for the study of inheritance procedures and bilateral kinship principles. Through a series of complicated mechanisms and awkwardly phrased locutions, one Mesopotamian family seems to have found a "loophole" in the practice of partible inheritance and thereby the means to keep an estate intact.

The largest tablet in the collection, which contains not a single verb, is apparently of unique importance to the analysis of Mesopotamian habitational patterns. The nature of the text is described, family structures are delineated, and group living patterns in Old Babylonian Kish are discussed.

Library of Congress Card Number 82-70790

ISBN 0-89003-086-3 (paper)
0-89003-087-1 (cloth)

Undena Publications, P.O. Box 97, Malibu, CA 90265, U.S.A.

TABLE OF CONTENTS

LIST OF TABLES

LIST OF MAPS

LIST OF PLATES

LIST OF FIGURES

PREFACE AND ACKNOWLEDGMENTS

The idea of studying the published and unpublished Old Babylonian texts from Kish germinated as part of Yoffee's earlier research into aspects of the bureaucracy of the crown in the latter part of the OB period. As was noted in the preface to the published results of that work (Yoffee 1977a), the intention was to expand the narrow limits of that first inquiry into an investigation of political and economic change during the entire period as could be observed from the vantage point of a single city. Since texts either from Kish or directly relating to the history of Kish date from before the ascendancy of the "First Dynasty of Babylon", and are continually attested until the last kings of that dynasty, Kish seemed to provide the ideal provenience for the investigation. Furthermore, many of the documents previously studied by Yoffee could be shown to have come from Kish although they were acquired from dealers and their archaeological context was unknown (cf. Finkelstein 1972:1-2; Stol 1973:216). As the first step in this research program it was necessary to examine and, in as far as practical, to edit the unpublished tablets that had been excavated in Kish. Thus, a project was undertaken with Veysel Donbaz to copy the material recovered by de Genouillac in 1912 and now conserved in the Istanbul Arkeoloji Müzeleri. The benefits of this amicable cooperation were especially evident during the long review of the hundreds of fragments of tablets that comprise the Kish collection in Istanbul.

A first draft of the present monograph was completed in 1974 and was accepted by Giorgio Buccellati for incorporation in his *Bibliotheca Mesopotamica* series, then just being inaugurated. It has been entirely due to the fact that Yoffee was preoccupied by other duties that this long delay in revising that initial manuscript has ensued. Rather than postponing publication further, it has been decided not to attempt the comprehensive study of all the documents that was once envisioned. The various chapter-essays presented here, which deal with the more remarkable (and better preserved) texts, moreover, stand independently; integration of the data must be deferred to further publications.

Yoffee's studies during the summers of 1973 and 1974 in Istanbul were made possible by the award of a "Fellowship in Mesopotamian Studies" by the Baghdad Committee of the American Schools of Oriental Research. Yoffee would like to acknowledge as well a summer stipend granted by the National Endowment for the Humanities (1976) and a grant-in-aid from the American Council of Learned Societies (1979-80). These awards have enabled the work on the Kish materials (also in Oxford, cf. Yoffee 1977b) to be advanced and have provided the time and facilities needed to complete this study. We both want to express our gratitude to the (then) director of the Archaeological Museums of Istanbul, N. Dolunay, and the General Director of Museums and Antiquities in Turkey, H. Gürçay, for the opportunity to undertake this joint project. Also deserving our thanks are the current Acting Director in Istanbul, İsmail Hilmi Köse, and the General Director in Ankara, Nurettin Yardımcı. Finally, we want to acknowledge M. Gallery's helpful critique of an early draft of the entire manuscript, M. Stol's generosity in providing lexical notes to Chapter 3, and I. J. Gelb's contribution to the understanding of the unusual document presented in Chapter 5.

For references, see below 1.4. Abbreviations are those of R. Borger, *Handbuch der Keilschriftliteratur*, vol. 1, Repertorium der sumerischen und akkadischen Texte. Walter de Gruyter, Berlin (1967).

CHAPTER 1

INTRODUCTION

1.1. The Kish Texts in Istanbul

As the first city to attain pre-eminence after the deluge according to the Sumerian King List, the venerability of Kish and the importance of the "Kish tradition" in early Mesopotamian cultures is well known to modern scholars (cf. Gelb 1977:14). It was, arguably, the unification of Sumer and Akkad by Sargon, who began his ascendancy to political power from Kish, that marked the historical reference point for all subsequent political aspirations of Mesopotamian kings. In spite of this importance of Kish in Mesopotamian historiographic thought, we must note that the city itself, notwithstanding its tendentiously conceived dominion as expressed in the Sumerian King List, in fact seems never to have been the seat of any long-lived political authority. Most texts that refer to Kish, moreover, do not come from that city (Yoffee 1977b).

Originally having been attracted to the ruins of Kish by the search to trace the boundaries of Babylon, scholars soon came to the site for its own sake because of the city's importance in the ancient texts themselves (Langdon 1924:Ch. 4; Gibson 1972a; Moorey 1978). Once the modern mound of Uhaimir was established as part of ancient Kish (Thureau-Dangin 1909), the ruins did not long evade systematic archaeological attention. In 1912, from January 23 to April 30, the Abbé Henri de Genouillac undertook a season of excavations. His aims were to elucidate the character of the buildings beneath several of the mounds which comprise the site and to recover the written records of the history and culture of the inhabitants of the city.

In the latter task de Genouillac was moderately successful, unearthing about 1400 tablets, most dating to the Old Babylonian period (de Genouillac 1924:20). These tablets were sent to Istanbul and thence the best preserved examples to Paris (de Genouillac 1924:20 and n. 1; Kupper 1959:19). Due to the onset of World War I and its aftermath de Genouillac was unable to return to Istanbul until 1924, whereupon he prepared the first volume of his *Premières recherches archéologiques à Kich* (*PRAK*). The second volume appeared the following year.

In *PRAK* I de Genouillac presented a twenty page description of the excavation itself and some of the goals he had set for the campaign. He noted that his single season was not entirely successful in fulfilling these goals, but that subsequent intended seasons were rendered impossible by forces beyond his control (1924:29). Also contained in *PRAK* I are the plans of the excavations and an "inventaire des objets." The largest section of the volume, however, consists of a list of tablets of the "B series," numbering 471 pieces of which 235 were copied by the author. Copies of five of the "A series" and four of the "O series" texts were also included. These three series of tablets, A, B, and O, are all conserved in Istanbul. De Genouillac's copies have been the subject of some criticism (Borger 1967: 151) and may have been executed in a very brief period of time. It may be said in de Genouillac's defense, however, that the copies at least fairly reflect the very fragmentary condition of the tablets themselves (in Istanbul).

PRAK II contains remarks on the reliefs, figurines, and ceramics recovered by the expedition. Some of de Genouillac's comments, especially on the ceramics, have held up rather well in the light of modern research on the archaeology of Kish (Gibson 1972a:70 and n. 39; Moorey 1966:24). Also included in this volume is an inventory of objects conserved in Paris and an incomplete diary of the excavations. The major part of this volume is devoted, however, as was the case in *PRAK* I, to the catalogues and copies of the tablets. The "A series," 590 texts in Istanbul, and described by de Genouillac as "ayant le moins d'intérêt" (1925:45) are only briefly listed. They are the most fragmentary of the materials excavated from Kish. The arrangement into "series" appears to depend solely on their condition of preservation, not any criterion of subject, date, or provenience. The C and D series, brought by de Genouillac to Paris, and thus published in *PRAK* II, consist of the "meilleurs documents trouvés à El 'Akhymer" (1925:34). Texts in these series include Old Babylonian letters, some contracts, and, most importantly (to de Genouillac), the Sumerian "religious" texts. Series C, 143 tablets, and Series D, 63 texts, were all copied by de Genouillac. Three texts from the O series were also copied in *PRAK* II, and the volume concludes with several seal inscriptions and an ancient houseplan with inscribed dimensions.

The allocation of a text to Istanbul or Paris was based simply on considerations of the putative importance of the text at hand and on its state of preservation. In Paris the criterion for separating C and D series seems utterly arbitrary. In Istanbul the A and B collections were designated only according to the relative condition of the tablets, the A series consisting of the most mutilated texts and the smallest fragments.

The great majority of the tablets unearthed by de Genouillac at Kish came from an area to the west of the ziggurat at Uhaimir (1924:19-20). This area included some house ruins of the Old Babylonian period and perhaps a scribal school associated with the ziggurat complex (de Genouillac 1924:23; Gibson 1972a:69). Although de Genouillac clearly regarded the recovery of tablets to be one of the most important aspects of his campaign, he showed no concern to mark the precise location of the texts. It is only from a passing remark that we learn that most of the scholastic texts–syllabaries, mathematical tables, and the like–may have come from an area rather nearer the ziggurat than from the area in which the letters and administrative texts were recovered.

> Deux points me semblent demander une mention spéciale: un groupe de chambres, assez voisin de la ziggourat, particulièrement fertile en tablettes scolaires (texts religieux, exercises d'écriture, syllabaires, tables de calcul) . . .
>
> (de Genouillac 1924:23).

Since the tablets were apportioned only according to their state of preservation and estimation of inherent importance, all opportunity for combining information on the character of their find-spots with that from the texts themselves has been lost (cf. Gibson 1972a, 1972b; Michalowski 1978 for a similar predicament arising from the later Anglo-American digs).

De Genouillac also excavated a section of a neo-Babylonian building in "East Kish" (Tell Ingharra), but apparently found few tablets there (Moorey 1978:13). This contrasts with the large quantity of texts, many dating to the Old Babylonian period, that the subsequent Oxford-Field Museum teams turned up at Ingharra. A comparison of the texts recovered from East and West Kish will await the publication of the materials now conserved in Oxford. It is ironic that the first publication by Langdon of the Anglo-American expedition's finds from the 1923 season, begun eleven years after the French campaign, actually appeared a few months prior to the publication of *PRAK* I. Langdon commented briefly on the work of de Genouillac, noting especially the work done at Ingharra (Langdon 1924: 54-55). De Genouillac, in reply, expressed his displeasure with the newly-undertaken expedition to Kish just as the first report of his own campaign was going to press (de Genouillac 1924:29 with ns. 2-3).

The texts from the not inappropriately named "ville d'Hammourapi" (the area west of the ziggurat at Uhaimir) include letters, administrative documents, Sumerian literary texts, and scraps of scholarly compendia. Of these texts the best studied have been the letters. Those in Paris have been collated and edited by Kupper (1959) whilst those in Istanbul have been published in transliteration by Kraus (1972). Since de Genouillac had copied all the texts brought to Paris, it would seem desirable, for the sake of completeness, to include here copies of all the remaining uncopied Istanbul texts of the "B series," to copy the entire "A series," and to remark on the copies provided by de Genouillac. This task, however worthwhile it may seem in the abstract, would have required the expenditure of time and energy far beyond the expectation of any analytical gain: the collection of more than 1100 items of these two series consists almost wholly of bits and pieces. The texts presented here, therefore, reflect, on the one hand, the more legible examples in the collection, and, on the other, our own historical reasons for having undertaken the study.

Since the intended investigation of socio-economic change during the Old Babylonian period in Kish must inevitably rely on information culled from dated administrative and private economic documents and letters, we have decided to publish (or in some cases republish when warranted) in hand-copy all these types of texts in the Istanbul collection. We have also included undated and/or broken texts that refer to officials and activities from which at least a hint of their context may be gained. (Other, disparate bits of data and names [and parts of names] have been recorded in our working notes so as to be employed in further studies of the Kish materials where appropriate.) In this manner almost all texts with more than a line or two of discernable economic or administrative content are presented in this volume. In Chapters 3-5 some of the more significant tablets are discussed in greater length. Occasional corrections of errors in the copies and inventory lists in the *PRAK* volumes are included when pertinent to our specific discussions.

1.2. An Outline of the History of Kish in the Old Babylonian Period

Since the Kish texts in Istanbul presented here were chosen partly for their historical import, it will be appropriate at the outset to sketch the political history (and some of the sources for the history) of Kish in the Old Babylonian period. A fuller examination of these disparate sources, including a full catalogue of kings, their dates, and an evaluation of the contents of the Kish texts, the vast majority of which are not part of the collection in Istanbul, must be deferred to later studies.

De Genouillac chose to excavate at Kish, stimulated in part by Thureau-Dangin's discussion of seven tablets said to have come from Uhaimir and an inscription of Ašduniyarim, king of Kish, but to whose reign no tablet yet recovered is dated (Thureau-Dangin 1911, in which this king's name is written *aš-du-ni-a-ri-im*; in a duplicate, *CT* 36 4:1, it is *aš-du-ni-e-ri-im*; for the reading, cf. Gelb 1961:270, note to p. 130f). These texts were in fact acquired by de Genouillac himself (1924:10), purchased from a dealer who claimed their provenience was Uhaimir (Thureau-Dangin 1911:68). Since some of these texts contained oaths sworn by Zababa, patron deity of Kish, Thureau-Dangin first concluded that modern Uhaimir was indeed the site of ancient Kish (Thureau-Dangin 1909). The importance of Kish in the third millennium and the imposing size of the ruins (at least twenty mounds, cf. Gibson 1972a: 58) prompted de Genouillac's interest in the site.

As previously noted, the Old Babylonian tablets recovered by de Genouillac came from an area that was chiefly residential, but may have also been the location of a "school." The excavator believed that this very area was the origin of the tablets acquired and published prior to his expedition to the site (de Genouillac 1924:19-20). In addition to those texts edited by Thureau-Dangin, these publications included tablets described briefly by Johns (1910; 1911). These tablets were said to have come from Kish (Johns 1910:279) and indeed referred to the same kings who appeared in the texts published by Thureau-Dangin (i.e., Manana, Yawium, and Halium) as well as to still other kings. Thirty-one of the texts examined by Johns were copied and edited by Langdon (1911) and then acquired by the Royal Scottish Museum, Edinburgh (and have benefited recently from being recopied by Dalley [1979]). From these publications it was seen that most of the texts related to the business affairs of two individuals, Šumšunuwater, son of Gubba'idu, and Sissunawrat, son of Belum.

The Oxford-Field Museum expeditions to Kish also excavated in the Old Babylonian house ruins near the ziggurat in Uhaimir and indeed turned up many Old Babylonian documents. No tablets from either de Genouillac's or these later Anglo-American excavations, however, mention any king known from the texts published in 1911 (for the one exception, *PRAK* II: D 6, see below). Of those texts purchased from dealers, many contain oaths sworn by, or dated to, rulers of the "Manana-dynasty," kings who venerated the deity Nanna/Sin, not Zababa, patron deity of Kish. Although tablets dating to Yawium invariably do associate Zababa and that ruler in oaths, other tablets show that Yawium held power in Kish only by the grace of a coregent who came from a city to which Kish was dependent (see below). We may conclude that the texts discussed by Thureau-Dangin, Johns, and Langdon were not recovered from the pitted area which later claimed the attention of Western excavators. Texts mentioning names of rulers to whom Kish was subject likely come from the home-cities of those kings (see below).

Groups of texts dating to the "Manana-dynasty" were subsequently published by Nies and Keiser (1920), Hunter (1930), Lutz (1932), Goetze (1950), Gordon (1952), Rutten (1958; 1959; 1960), and Simmons (1960; 1961). Specific discussions of the kings and their cities that competed in the twin struggles for independence and dominion in the time just before and then during the reigns of the first two kings of the "First Dynasty of Babylon" have been offered by Kraus (1952-53), Kupper (1957:197-203), Edzard (1957:130-135), Simmons (1960:75-87), and Reiner (1961). Of these investigations the most comprehensive is that of Simmons who also pointed out that kings mentioned in texts published by Speleers (1925), Riftin (1937), and Grant (1938), among others, interacted in this struggle as did kings from cities on the Diyala (cf. Jacobsen 1940). After a time when little research seems to have been devoted to these subjects, Pomponio has recently published an interpretive essay on "la 'dinastia' di Mananâ" (1976) and Charpin has undertaken a rather larger project in connection with the publication of further materials in the Louvre that are from the same collection from which Rutten's tablets came (Charpin 1978a; 1978b). Although both essays usefully review the evidence (Charpin adding some new materials), many of the research steps of the older studies have been repeated and most of the same conclusions have been reached about the order and interconnections of the kings. Written at about the same time, the articles are not cross-referenced and differ mainly in the authors' attempts to localize the home-city of the "Manana-dynasty" kings. Both studies were also unable to incorporate materials newly published by Simmons (1978, but see now Charpin 1979) and those republished by Dalley (1979). Neither Pomponio nor Charpin extends his inquiries beyond those kings of the "Manana-dynasty" (Charpin includes Naqimum and Ahimaraṣ among these, whilst Pomponio does not), and consequently a number of texts and studies relating to the maelstrom of political alliances and evanescent hegemonies in which these rulers were engulfed are passed over (e.g., Leemans 1966; al-'Adami 1967; Renger 1970). Recent publications by Greengus on Diyala texts (1979, with references to previous articles on texts from Eshnunna, Khafajah, Harmal, Dhiba'i) and Kienast of Kisurra tablets (1978), as well as the short note by Yoffee (1977b) reporting on Kish tablets, were unavailable to Pomponio and Charpin (partly rectified in Charpin 1979). It may be observed that by focusing solely on the kings of the "Manana-dynasty" there must be a tendency toward oversimplifying the complex interactions and shifting alliances that took place among many cities over a rather large area (see also Charpin 1979). It may also be noted that the texts dated by kings of the "Manana-dynasty" have not been examined for purposes other than their chronological and archival significance. It will not be the aim of the present historical outline, however, to assemble all the disparately published data available for political and institutional investigations in this period. Rather, we shall simply take up those matters that allow us to place the Kish texts in Istanbul within the historical parameters that will be appropriate to these continuing inquiries.

Manana (for this name cf. Reiner 1961:121), mentioned in the dates and/or oaths of more than seventy texts, including both published and unpublished examples, is the most frequently attested of the rulers of Kish before the ascendancy of Babylonian domination there. Both Simmons (1960:87) and Pomponio (1976:293) assign him fifteen regnal years; Charpin counts fourteen (1978:29). Manana was a contemporary of Sumu'abum since the date of that king's thirteenth year appears in at least ten texts, all from the archive of Šumšunuwatar, one of which contains an oath by Nanna and Manana (Thureau-Dangin 1911: no. 1). In *TIM* 6 (van Dijk 1978): no. 38 Manana is invoked again in an oath whilst the tablet is dated to Sumu'abum 3. Most of the Manana year-names record dedications to the temple of Nanna, although Amurrum is also venerated by him.

Another contemporary of Manana was Yawium, local ruler of Kish. In one text (Langdon 1911: no. 7; see now Dalley 1978: no. 37), whose date is lost, the oath is sworn by Nanna and Manana and by Zababa and Yawium. In two texts (Thureau-Dangin 1911: no. 4; Langdon 1911: no. 5) the oath is sworn by Zababa and Yawium whilst the date is Sumula'el's sixth year-name (or possibly Sumu'abum's second). Yet another contemporary is Halium, for in two texts (Simmons 1960: no. 123; Simmons 1978: no. 111) the oath records Nanna and Halium alongside Zababa and Yawium. Halium seems to have ruled at the time of a defeat of Urninurta of Isin since the year-name mu ur-^{d}ninurta ba-gaz appears in a text dated to Halium (oath by Nanna and Halium). One more ruler who can be correlated with Yawium is Sumuditan(a) since an oath is sworn by Zababa and Yawium is a tablet dated "the year Sumuditan died" (Thureau-Dangin 1911: no. 3). Sumuditan(a) is the only one of all these rulers so far discussed (with the exception of Sumula'el) to appear on a tablet that was actually excavated in Kish. This text, published by de Genouillac in *PRAK* II (D 6), records the construction of the "great ship of Ilabrat" and contains an oath by Lugalmarad and Sumuditan. Persons appearing in the contract can be traced in a text edited by Simmons (1960: no. 127) in which the oath is also sworn by Lugalmarad and Sumuditan. Since Urninurta died two years before Sumu'abum's first regnal year in Babylon, Yawium seems to have ruled in Kish during the entire reign of that Babylonian king, but under the dominion of Halium and then Manana (and perhaps also under an intermediate king, Abdi'arah, also of their home-city. For discussion of Abdi'arah, king of Khafajah, see Charpin 1978a: 23, 26-27).

From these synchronisms it follows that Yawium must have been a rather long-lived ruler in Kish, but that his durability was tied to his willingness to submit to the power of rival kings. The time after the collapse of the "Third Dynasty of Ur" was characterized by a condition of extreme political flux with competing leaders intermittently extending their authority over cities temporarily rendered vassals. In this welter of shifting confederations and in the absence of long-lasting power, Kish seems to have stood out, by virtue of its historic prestige, as a symbol of regional control and political legitimation. Like Nippur in the south, Kish was known not for exercising power but for representing it.

It will not be appropriate here to delineate the order and synchronisms of the kings and cities which competed more or less equally in the early part of the Old Babylonian period. Tables of such synchronisms may be found in Pomponio (1976:293-294), Charpin (1978a: 40), Kienast (1978:38-39), Simmons (1978:26-28; note Manabalte'el is a king of Kisurra, not Sippar; Ibnišadum is a king of Marad); and Greengus (1979:23). Concerning the political situation in Kish itself, the version of Simmons (1960:87) has remained substantially unchanged in these newer tabulations. (For the convenience of the discussion we simply provide a table of kings mentioned in this chapter and a table of key events. Maps are included to indicate the locus of these historical interactions.)

In reckoning "kings of Kish" during the early Old Babylonian period we must deal with the following types of political situations:

(1) Independent local ruler. (Example:) Yawium issues his own date-formula commemorating pious acts on behalf of the patron deity of Kish, Zababa (e.g., Langdon 1911: no. 14). In contracts oaths are sworn solely by Zababa and Yawium (e.g., Thureau-Dangin 1911: no. 3). Both the cited documents are from the "archive" of Ṣissunawrat.

(2) Coregency. (Example a:) The local ruler of Kish acknowledges the vassalage of his city to another ruler. Thus, Yawium and Zababa appear in oaths after the name of the patron deity and king of the conquering city (e.g., after Nanna and Halium, Simmons 1978:111; after Nanna and Manana, Langdon 1911: no. 7). A year-date of the local coregent, Yawium (e.g., Simmons 1978:111), appearing after such a double-oath, might indicate the relative power actually exercised in Kish. (Example b:) A second type of subservience to a non-native ruler of Kish is indicated by texts in which the oath is sworn by Zababa and Yawium whilst the year-date is that of the foreigner (e.g., Thureau-Dangin 1911: no. 4, date of Sumula'el or Sumu'abum). In this case we may be witnessing Sumula'el's first attempt to wield power in Kish, that is, only on a limited scale. It may be inferred that this policy was not entirely successful for Sumula'el records defeating Kish in his thirteenth year-name and destroying its walls in his nineteenth. (Example c:) A text from an "archive" known to document activities in Kish ("archive" of Ṣissunawrat) contains the oath by a non-local king, Abdi'arah, and his divine patron, Nanna, and also the year-date of that king (e.g., Langdon 1911: no. 4; cf. Dalley 1979, pl. 39).

By similar estimation it can be seen that some texts mentioning "kings of Kish" may not come from Kish. Tablets that are from Kish are those (1) dated by native rulers; or (2) dated by native rulers, but whose oath is sworn also by a foreign king; or (3) dated to, and sworn by, a foreign king—but whose contents reveal its locus to be Kish. In this last instance, however, it is obvious that many texts assigned to a king who conquered Kish may also have come from his home-city. A further complication arises since a foreign "king of Kish" may have conquered other cities in addition to having dominion in Kish. Lastly, a foreign power like Babylon conquered both Kish and the home-city of a king who ruled as coregent there (e.g., as is seen in texts whose oath is sworn by Manana but whose year-date is that of Sumu'abum).

Table 1. Select List of Kings of the Early Old Babylonian Period Cited in Chapter 1

Babylon	Sippar	Marad-Kazallu	KISH	(Ilip?)	Diyala	Larsa	Isin	Kisurra
			Ašduniyarim				Urninurta (1923-1896)	
		Sumuditan	Yawium	Halium				
Sumuʾabum (1894-1881)				Abdiʾarah	Abdiʿarah	Sumuʾel (1894-1866)		
								Sumuʾabum (in oath)
				Manana				
	Ilummaʾila	Alumbiumu						
Sumulaʾel (1880-1845)								
		Sumunumhim			Hammidušur			
				Sumuyamutbal				
				Manium				

Table 2. Key Events in Early Old Babylonian History

ca.	1920 (?)	Ašduniyarim, independent ruler in Kish
		Urninurta defeated; Halium independent
	1910	Sumuditan of Marad ruling in Kish
		Yawium, independent ruler in Kish
	1900	Halium, coregent with Yawium in Kish
		Manana, coregent with Yawium in Kish
	1893	Sumuʾabum in Dilbat
	1892	Sumuʾabum, coregent in city of Manana
	1891	Sumuʾel of Larsa defeats Kazallu and Akuṣum
		Manana rebuilds wall of Akuṣum
	1884	Sumuʾel defeats army of Kish (which had attacked Larsa?)
	1882	Sumuʾabum takes Kazallu and defeats an army of Larsa (in Kazallu area?)
		Sumuʾabum briefly in Kisurra (date uncertain)
	1878	Sumulaʾel defeats Alumbiumu of Marad (in struggle over Dilbat)
	1874	Sumulaʾel, coregent in Kish
	1874	Sumuʾel defeats Kazallu
	1868-62	Sumulaʾel campaigns and finally takes Kish
	1861	Sumulaʾel takes Marad-Kazallu
	1855	Sumulaʾel takes Kutha
	1849	Sumulaʾel, coregent in city of Manana

Maps: Introductory Notes and Sources

Map 1: Cities and Hypothesized Watercourses in the Ur III Period.
Source: Edzard and Farber 1974
Note: The course of the Euphrates through Sippar, Kish, and Nippur follows the reconstruction suggested by Jacobsen (1960) based on textual references of its location.
Key:
- ● confirmed location
- ○ unconfirmed location
- ▲/△ confirmed/unconfirmed seat of Ur III provincial governor (ensí)
- ■/□ confirmed/unconfirmed seat of Ur III military governor (šagin)

Map 2: Settlements and Hypothetical Watercourses in the Old Babylonian and Kassite Periods.
Source: Gibson 1972a, map 5 (cf. Adams 1959)
Note: No watercourse is hypothesized connecting Sippar, Kish, and Nippur since the Old Babylonian sites lying on watercourses follow a line to the east of Kish. The location of site no. 248 (Gibson 1972a, map 4) which has been postulated by Charpin as Ilip (see text) has been added.

Map 3: Old Babylonian Cities.
Note: Map is not to scale.

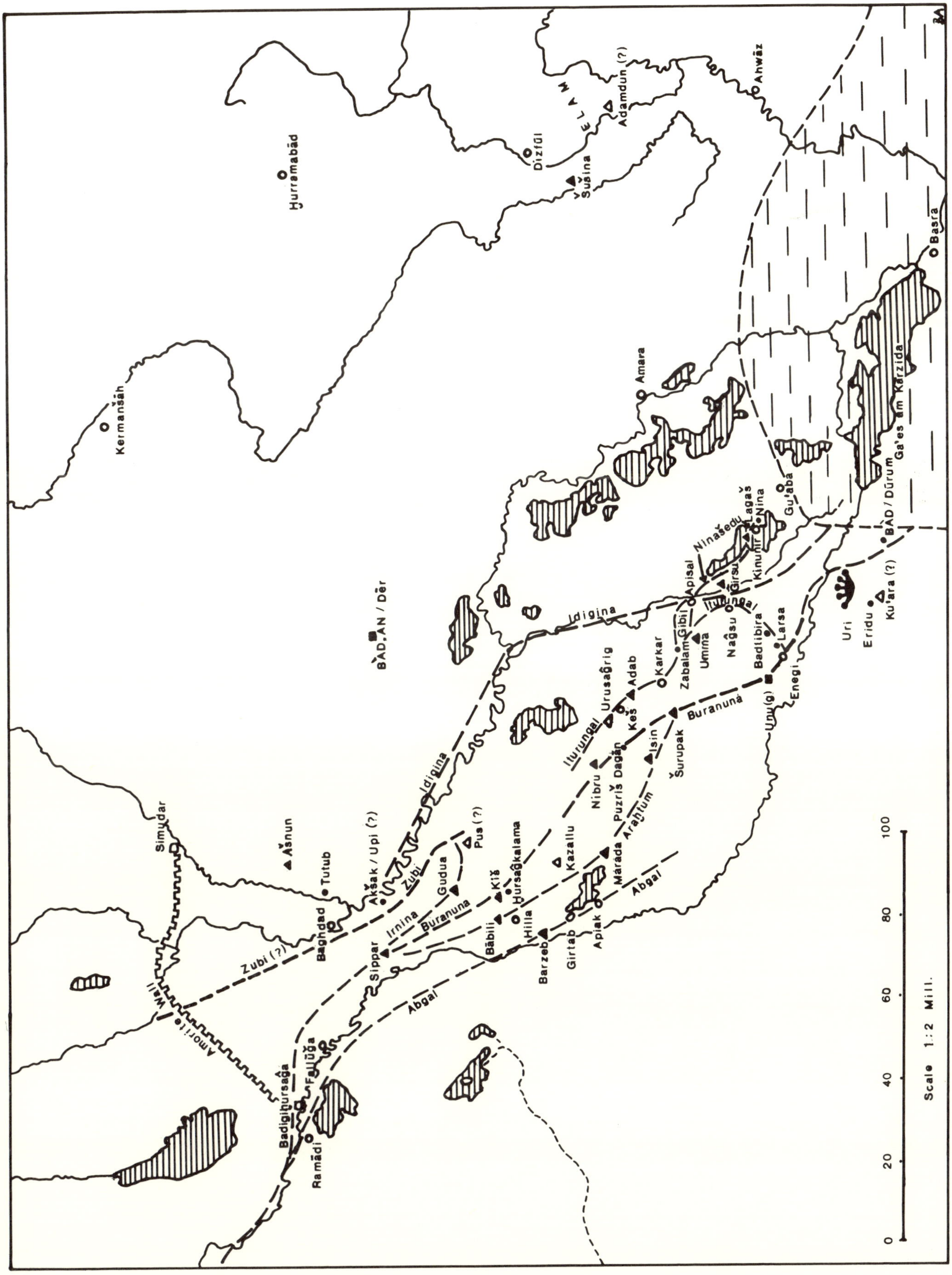

Map 1. Cities and Hypothesized Watercourses in the Ur III Period.

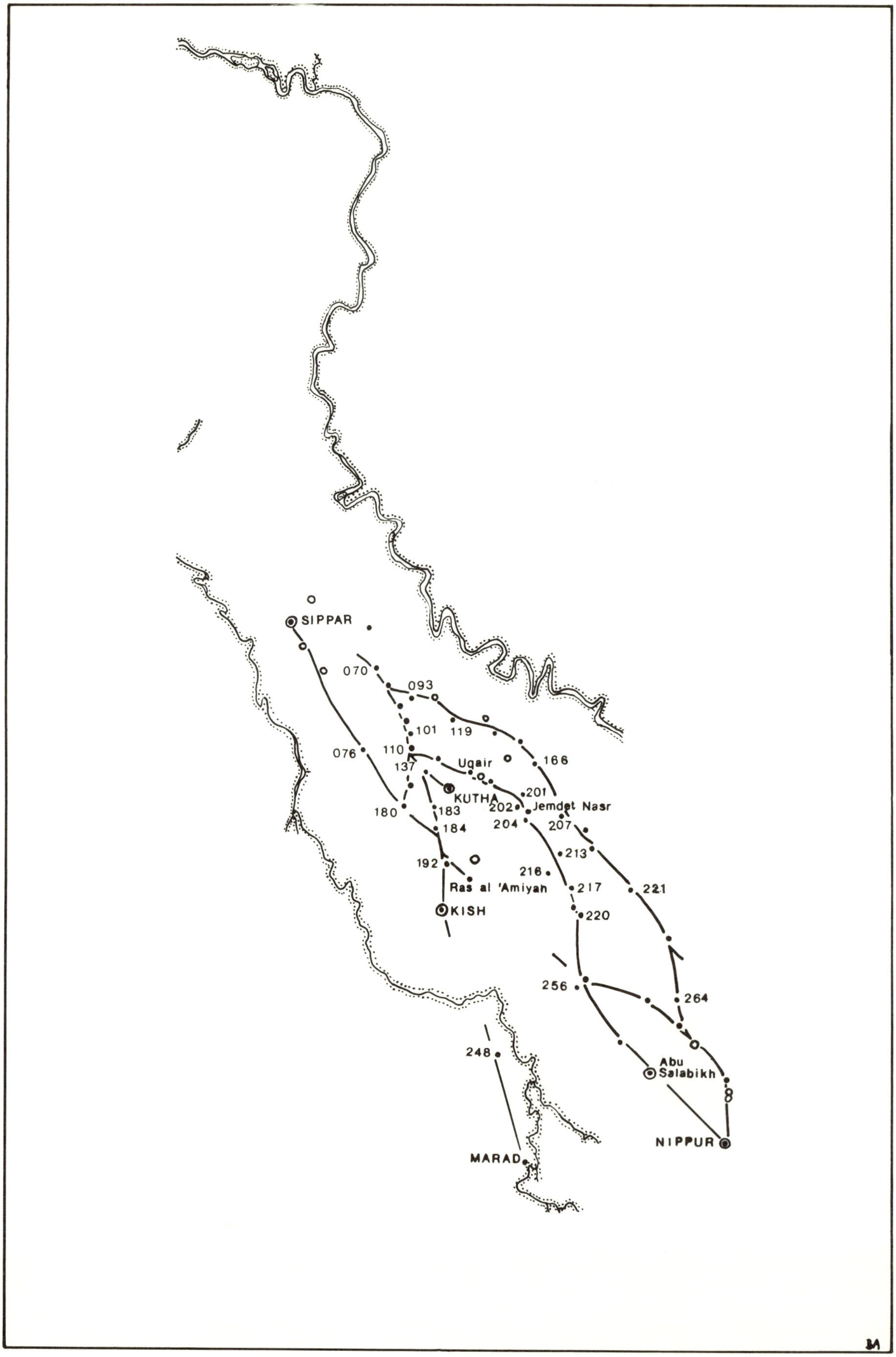

Map 2. Settlements and Hypothetical Watercourses in the Old Babylonian and Kassite Periods.

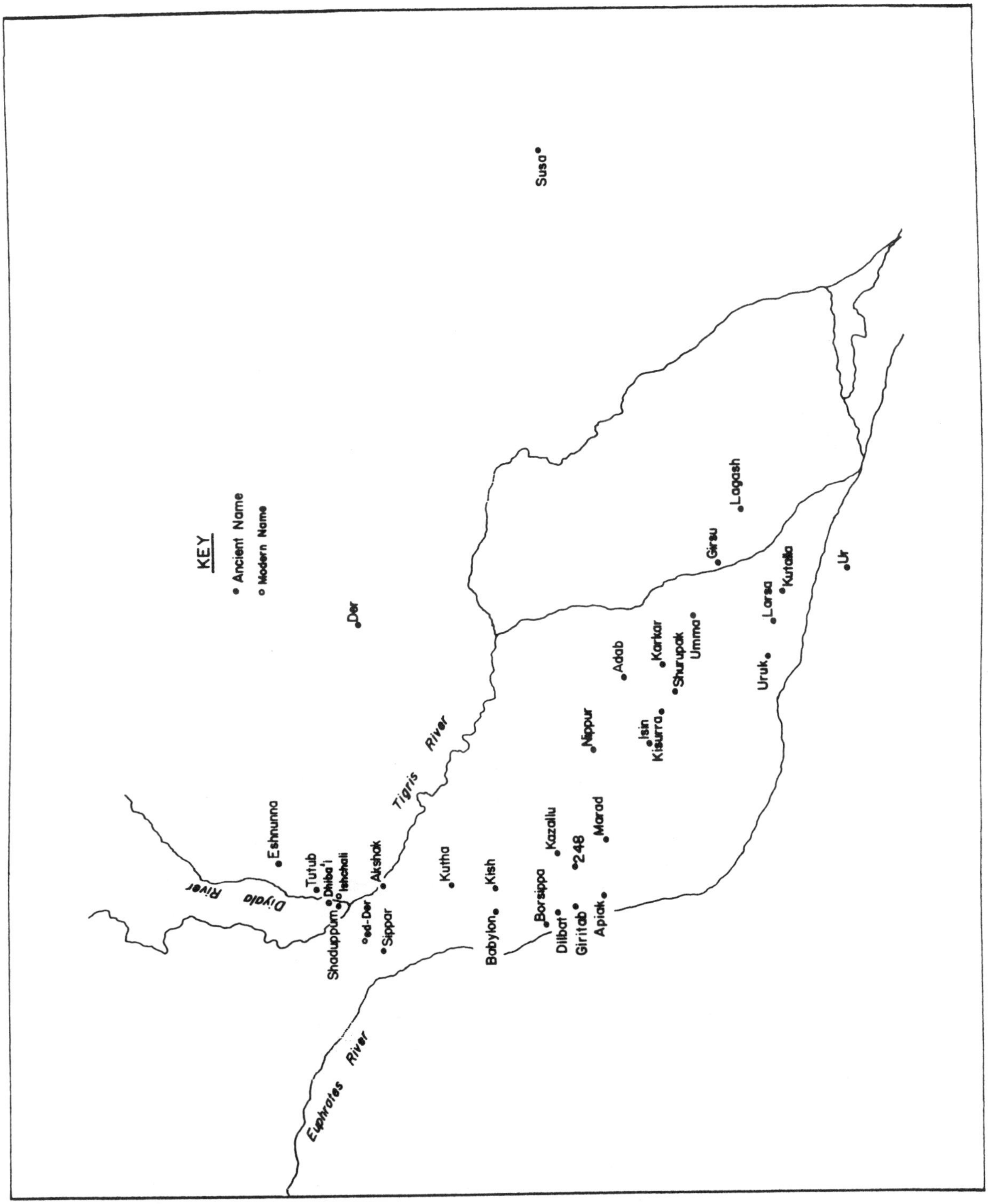

Map 3. Old Babylonian Cities.

The matter of identifying the home-cities of these foreign "kings of Kish" has inevitably been approached by comparing the gods connected in oaths alongside the kings, and commemorated in their year-dates, with cities (known from divine hymns, temple hymns, god-lists, etc.) in which these gods were especially venerated. The comparisons are not straightforward for two reasons. First, several deities may be associated with a single king. Thus, Sumuditan(a) appears in oaths with Lugalmarad, patron deity of Marad, and with Numušda of Kazallu. Numušda most often appears in that king's year-names, but is not exclusively honored in them. In an unpublished text in the Ashmolean Museum, the date commemorates a temple of Numušda but in the catalogue the provenience is said to be Marad. Since Marad and Kazallu are nearby cities and historically connected (cf. Kraus 1955), this sort of politico-religious interrelationship between the two is not unexpected. But since it is also usual for a conquering ruler to (try to) legitimize his presence in subject cities by respecting their patron divinities, there can be no simple correlation between the god(s) mentioned in a year-date or oath and the home-city of the king under whose jurisdiction the document is recorded.

In the second instance, localizing the home-city of the "Manana-dynasty" kings has involved the difficulty of connecting a particular city with the worship of Nanna/Sin, a divinity of the "Reichspantheon" and thus honored to some extent in all Mesopotamian cities. Three attempts at an identification may be reported here. Simmons (1960:79) suggested Kutha, a large mound northeast of Babylon and well-known as an important place in the Old Babylonian period. Since a tablet published by Gordon (1952: no. 38) was said to have been found at Kutha, and this text was related to others published by Rutten that date to the "Manana-dynasty" kings, and, one suspects, because of Kutha's undoubted importance in this period and location near Kish and Babylon, Simmons was inclined to favor that site as the home-city of Manana. Although acknowledging that the patron deity of Kutha was Nergal, Simmons cites "evidence that Nanna was also worshipped there" (Simmons 1960:79). The suggestion is not convincing, not least because Nergal *never* appears in any oaths or year-dates of any of the rulers of the "Manana-dynasty."

Pomponio (1976) has tentatively proffered Lagaba as Manana's seat of power. Having excluded other possibilities, he notes that many Lagaba texts have in fact been found (cf. Leemans 1960), although they date exclusively to the time of Hammurabi and Samsu'iluna. In an inscription of Samsu'iluna that king reports having rebuilt the wall of Lagaba and dedicating it to Nanna. Further, on the basis of prosopography Lagaba ought to be in the vicinity of Kish, Kutha, and Sippar. Although Pomponio's "identification" is put forward with all due scholarly caution, there is obviously very little positive evidence that Lagaba is the city in question.

Charpin's arguments for localizing the home-city of the "Manana-dynasty" as Ilip are more ingenious and his confidence seems undiminished for their circumstantial nature. In the collection of "Sumerian temple hymns" (Sjöberg and Bergmann 1969), besides Ur (which is too far south for any continuous interaction in northern Babylonian politics) as a center of worship of Nanna is the city Urum. This place, not found in Old Babylonian documents, is taken by Charpin (1978a:16-17) as the Wurumu of the northern revolt against Naramsin (which included Kazallu, Marad, Eshnunna, Kish, and Sippar [cf. Grayson and Sollberger 1976]). Now, in the *Malku* and *HAR-gud* lexical lists, a town *ú-ru* is equated as *ì-lip* / *i-lip*, a place which does occur in texts throughout the Old Babylonian period. Indeed, Sumu'abum's third year-name reads "the year the wall of Ilip (often spelled KI.BAL.MAŠ.DÀ) was taken." The "kingdom of Ilip" is further considered by Charpin to incorporate three other towns, Dunnum, SAG.DA.IN.PÀD, and Akuṣum. The evidence for this is that each of them is mentioned in the year-names of Manana, Sumuyamutbal, and Manana, respectively, as having its city-wall built by those kings. Akuṣum is thought by Charpin to be the name of two separate towns since he does not regard a "Subarian" Akuṣum to be the place otherwise known to be in the vicinity of Babylon (Charpin 1978a:19-20; but cf. Finkelstein 1955:3, n. 29). However, Charpin (rightly) does not admit that there were two towns named Damrum (HI.GAR^{ki}), which is also thought to be in the vicinity of Kish and a place in which Sin was venerated: "Du fait de sa localisation et de la présence de Sin comme divinité principale, la ville de Damrum pourrait être envisagée comme capitale de Manana" (Charpin 1978a:19, n. 29). Opposed to previous views that Ilip lay between Sippar and Kutha (Edzard 1976:52; Reiner 1961:124; Sjöberg and Bergmann 1976:138), Charpin locates the site in the Kish-Marad-Dilbat district. In fact, by consulting Adams' site survey of this region (1972), Charpin concludes that site no. 248 (previously thought by Adams [1959] to have been Kazallu) "correspond exactement à celle que nous recherchons pour Ilip" (1978a:22). Adams describes the surface remains on that site, however, as indicating an occupation there in the Uruk through Larsa periods and again in Achaemenid-Parthian times, but not throughout the Old Babylonian period (1972:205). The site does not appear on map 5, "Settlements and Hypothetical Watercourses in the Old Babylonian and Cassite Periods" at all (see map 2 above), although it does turn up on map 4 for the Akkadian-Ur III-Isin/Larsa periods (Charpin confusingly cites "cartes 2 à 9"). Further inspection of Adams' survey shows several unidentified "cities" in the area from ʿAqar Quf to Marad and no less than eighteen unidentified "towns" of the size of Marad (Adams 1972:186).

From the information recorded in the year-dates of the major powers, an outline of the political vicissitudes during the early part of the Old Babylonian period, including the struggle for control of Kish, may be reconstructed. Although the respective local situations were far from secure, the campaigns of the rulers of Babylon and Larsa in the early 19th century B.C. seem to prefigure the later full-scale warfare between the two cities and the northern and southern confederations led by their kings Hammurabi and Rimsin. Sumuʾabum of Babylon and Sumuʾel of Larsa acceded to their respective thrones in the same year (1894, according to the middle chronology). In his third year-name Sumuʾabum records taking the wall of Ilip. In Sumuʾel's fourth year-name he notes a victory over Kazallu and Akuṣum (cf. Walters 1973). In his eleventh year-name Sumuʾel commemorates his victory over an army of Kish, and in his twenty-second formula, his victory over Kazallu. Sumuʾabum had previously taken Kazallu nine years before (thirteenth year-name), the same year in which many tablets are dated which contain oaths sworn by Manana. In one of Manana's year-names he himself reports having rebuilt the wall of Akuṣum. Finally, an oath of Sumuʾabum (who is associated with Ninurta and is himself deified) appears in a tablet from the southern city of Kisurra (Kienast 1978: no. 93). It may thus be seen that Larsa's push to the north brought it directly into conflict with Babylon's southward expansion. Although Babylon and Larsa were but two of many cities competing for wider dominion during the early 19th century B.C., the local history of Kish must also be perceived in this larger, and ultimately more important, political context.

The roots of Sumuʾabum, founder of the Amorite "First Dynasty of Babylon," are obscure (cf. Edzard 1957:122). On the basis of his veneration of Nanna/Sin, he has even been connected with kings of the "Manana-dynasty" (Edzard 1957:121, n. 644; Reiner 1961:123), although indications of this (mention of Nanna in two year-dates) are hardly overwhelming. It has also been observed that Sumuʾabum was not always considered by later kings of Babylon to be the antecedent of their dynasty since kings traced their descent in some instances only to Sumulaʾel (Edzard 1957:112; however, cf. Finkelstein 1966, a genealogical reckoning which does include Sumu abum). Sumuʾabum, although campaigning far beyond the territory immediately controlled by Babylon, seems to have exercised little direct control outside the capital and was only able to achieve an imperfect mechanism of coregencies with local rulers of nearby cities. Published letters from ed-Der indeed indicate that his successor on the Babylonian throne, Sumulaʾel, was a contemporary and possible rival of his (al-ʿAdami 1967: pl. 17, IM 49537; Edzard 1970:15-16).

It is Sumulaʾel who must be considered the architect of the power enjoyed by the later kings of the "First Dynasty." In his third year-name he records a victory over "Halambu," probably a king of Marad who threatened Babylon's previously acquired control over Dilbat (Simmons 1960:86; Leemans 1966). From the ed-Der letters (al-ʿAdami 1967: pl. 1, IM 49341) we learn that this "Halambu" (=Alumbiumu) was also a rival of Sumuʾabum. Indeed, Marad plays a significant role in the struggle for political supremacy in the region around Kish at this time (Yoffee 1977c). Sumuditan(a), upon whose death Yawium of Kish was able to establish a short-lived independence for his city, was either from Marad or Kazallu (see above). Sumulaʾel first effected a coregency with Yawium for that Babylonian's sixth year-date is attested in Kish (if the year-date is not that of Sumuʾabum's second year). Babylonian dominion did not extend far to the south, however, since in Sumulaʾel's seventh regnal year Sumuʾel of Larsa claims to have defeated an army from Kazallu. Indeed, as was the case under the Ur III kings (Kraus 1955), the area about Marad-Kazallu-Apiak can be regarded as the dividing line between southern and northern Babylonia and was the scene of most of the military action undertaken by competing kings in the early 19th century B.C.

In his thirteenth through nineteenth year-dates, Sumulaʾel was able to succeed in finally ending (by force) the ambitions of the local rulers of Kish. Marad was brought into the Babylonian orbit by his nineteenth regnal year, since a tablet found in Marad and whose oath is sworn by Lugalmarad and Sumulaʾel lists the Babylonian king's twentieth year-name (Speleers 1923: no. 232). That year-name, commemorating the destruction of the wall of Kazallu, shows Sumulaʾel's concern to secure the southern "border" of what he was forming into a northern Old Babylonian core area (cf. Renger 1970). In his twenty-sixth regnal year Sumulaʾel captured Kutha. About this time he was also in effective control of the home-city of the "Manana-dynasty", since he issued a *mīšarum*-edict jointly with Sumuyamutbal, probably successor of Manana (Simmons 1960:81; Reiner 1961:121-122). In a tablet from his twenty-sixth year the oath is sworn by Marduk and Sumulaʾel, Nanna and Sumuyamutbal (Goetze 1950:70). Other coregencies with rulers of Old Babylonian towns can also be dated to this time (e.g., Veenhof 1973:375-377). The last king of the "Manana-dynasty", Manium, is attested in a text with Sumulaʾel's thirty-second year-name; he was presumably the last in his line.

Sumulaʾel's policy toward the south was to establish an alliance with Uruk. His daughter married Sinkašid of that southern city and subsequently an Uruk king, Anam, takes pains to remind his Babylonian contemporary that they are of "one house" (Falkenstein 1963; cf. Yoffee 1978:23, with ns. 16-17). In addition to his northern conquests he was careful to rebuild the walls of subject cities and to dedicate temples to their gods. Although we cannot discern the details of his activities, the honor paid him by his descendants is eloquent testimony to their effect. From a city originally no more than one among many equally competing powers, he forged a region that became closely tied to the capital in systems of political and economic policy. It was from this stable core that Hammurabi directed his dramatic military victories and established a pan-Babylonian dominion, however ephemerally, that had not been seen since Sargon. It was this core that continued to function as a single sociopolitical entity throughout the period of decline under the last northern Old Babylonian kings (cf. Yoffee 1977a).

These Babylonian rulers continued to venerate the ancient city of Kish as we learn from their year-names and royal inscriptions. In his thirty-sixth year-formula, Hammurabi notes having rebuilt the temples of Zababa and Ishtar in Kish, originally constructed by his great ancestor, Sumulaʾel. Samsuʾiluna's twenty-second and twenty-fourth year-dates commemorate his own building activities in Kish, and, indeed, a great many stamped and inscribed bricks of that ruler were located by Langdon (1924:15; Sollberger 1969; Borger 1958). Ammiṣaduqa's fifteenth year-name records his placement of a statue in the temple of Zababa in Kish. From a position of paramount importance for contesting powers during the early part of the Old Babylonian period, after the time of Sumulaʾel the destiny of Kish was inextricably and evermore tied to that of its powerful neighbor.

1.3. Dated Texts in Istanbul

Of the approximately 1400 tablets recovered by de Genouillac in Kish, the majority of which date to the Old Babylonian period, fifty-nine documents preserve year-names. Only two of these are not dated to kings of the "First Dynasty of Babylon." One dates to Šulgi's thirty-ninth year (*PRAK* 2: D 49–but is presumably a Dreham text), and the other may be ascribed to Sumuditan (see above) since he is mentioned in its oath. The latter tablet is the only one recovered from the expeditions to Kish that attests the presence there of any of the rival kings who competed for dominion in and before the time of Sumulaʾel of Babylon. Although a tablet dating to Yawium was reported by Langdon to have been found "in a chamber of the temple of Ilbaba" (Langdon 1924:13-14) and has also been mentioned by Gibson (1972a and n. 79), this tablet has not been located by Yoffee in the course of studying the Kish materials in Oxford. Gibson (personal communication) has informed us that a card from the original Oxford-Field Museum Expedition's files does note that the name "Japium-Ilum" appears on a tablet read by Langdon. This tablet, however, does not have an Ashmolean Museum number and apparently was never processed into the Ashmolean's collections. It may also be remarked that several other tablets from Kish that were even published by Langdon (1927) never reached the Ashmolean. The reference "Japium-Ilum" itself is enigmatic.

The earliest dated tablet in Istanbul, excluding the two cited above, is Ki 789 which records the building of the wall of Babylon. This year-name cannot be attributed with certainty to a particular king, since it served as the first year-name of Sumuʾabum, the fifth year-name of Sumulaʾel, and the second year-name of Apilsin. Since this date occurs in an ús-sa form in tablets whose oaths are sworn by Yawium (Thureau-Dangin 1911 no. 4; Langdon 1911: no. 5) and these are taken to date likeliest to the reign of Sumulaʾel, we have provisionally assigned a Sumulaʾel date also to Ki 789. At this time Sumulaʾel had not conquered Kish, but was recognized as the overlord of the local ruler, Yawium. That Sumulaʾel's dominion over Kish in his early years was by no means welcomed can be inferred from his thirteenth–seventeenth year-names, which record the "destruction" of Kish, and his nineteenth date, which relates the destruction of the wall of Kish. After Sumulaʾel's conquest, however, he was careful to portray himself as a just and legitimate ruler by rebuilding sacred places and honoring the local deities of subjugated cities (cf. Edzard 1957: 124; Langdon 1924:14-15). From the latter part of his reign texts bearing his thirty-second and thirty-third year-names were recovered in Kish. By this time Sumulaʾel had consolidated his power over much of the territory in northern Babylonia.

One document in Paris dates to the time of Sabium, son of Sumulaʾel, and from the reign of that king's successor, Apilsin, comes at least one text that is in Istanbul. Little is known of these rulers who administered the lands brought into the Babylonian "core" established by Sumulaʾel.

The most frequently attested king among the dated texts recovered by de Genouillac is Sinmuballit, son of Apilsin, and father of Hammurabi. The little-known career of this ruler must be reconstructed essentially on the basis of the information contained in his year-names. His first date, represented in Istanbul in two texts, commemorates the construction of a fortress (cf. Stol 1976:28 and n. 9) and is typical of his activities (cf. Edzard 1957:152-153). Sinmuballiṭ's eighth year-name also appears twice among the Istanbul texts and his eleventh year-name occurs sixteen times. Since all sixteen of these texts are from what we have termed "the bureau of brick-production at Kish" they are discussed in Chapter 3 below. The year-name itself, mu bàd IM^{ki} ^{d}EN.ZU-*mu-ba-li-iṭ* mu-un-dù-a in full (Horsnell 1974:154), means "the year Sinmuballiṭ built the wall of Karkar." The reading Karkar has recently been established and its location determined to be between Adab and Zabalam (Renger 1970). Sinmuballiṭ's fortification of this southern village, and that of the wall of Marad in his twelfth year-name, seem to symptomize some of the important political developments of this period. The reason Sinmuballiṭ undertook this military activity was his concern with the rising power of Rimsin of Larsa. Thus, he first attempted to strengthen the border area of the Babylonian "core." His southern policy, then, included not only fortifying towns to the south of this Babylonian territory, but also continuing Babylon's alliance with Uruk and even confronting Rimsin himself (Edzard 1957:153). Both documents and letters found in Kish (Kupper 1959 and below Chapter 3) show the close relationship between Kish and the capital during his reign.

Several Istanbul tablets date to kings Hammurabi and Samsuʾiluna, while only two bear year-names of Abiʾešuh. The last three kings of the "First Dynasty" are not represented among the tablets excavated by de Genouillac. In sum it may be stated that the area dug in 1912 was not inappropriately called by de Genouillac the "ville d'Hammourapi": the texts in Istanbul (and Paris) date in a cluster in the middle part of the Old Babylonian period.

If we have discussed a group of texts that refer to those kings who ruled Kish during the earliest part of the Old Babylonian period and have noted that the tablets recovered by the de Genouillac expedition date to the middle part of the period, we turn now briefly to those Kish documents that date to the last kings of the "First Dynasty of Babylon." Many of these texts are to be found in the *YOS* 13 volume published by Finkelstein (1972). As can be shown from references to Kish in some of these texts, to the cult of Zababa, by personal names compounded with that divinity, and by cross-referencing these categories, more than 100 documents in that volume may be said to come from Kish (Finkelstein 1972:7). All of these texts date to the time after Samsuʾiluna and the majority date to the very last kings of the "First Dynasty." Similar texts were previously published by Szlechter (1963) and before him by Fish (1952a; 1952b). These texts were originally acquired by Johns (1914) and not only belong to the same archives as do many of the texts in *YOS* 13 (cf. Finkelstein 1972:7 and n. 25), but were probably acquired from the same dealer. (The texts published by Speleers and glossed with the remark "Akymer" were in fact acquired from a different dealer by de Genouillac before he began his campaign at Kish [cf. Speleers 1925: I; de Genouillac 1924:10]). Texts from Kish that date to the late Old Babylonian period have also found their way to Berlin and have recently been published by Klengel (1971; 1973).

During the approximately 350-year span of time documented by the Old Babylonian texts from Kish, the structure and function of the political, economic, and social systems in the city changed markedly. In this volume, however, we do not offer a study of those changes. Rather, we publish those texts conserved in Istanbul which must serve as a prelude to that research. The contents of these texts are described in the catalogues that comprise Chapter 2. Those warranting lengthier comment are taken up in Chapters 3-5. Our analysis of these materials is naturally not ended with the publication of this monograph since future investigation of the history of Kish in the Old Babylonian period must incorporate these texts within a more comprehensive analytical framework than is appropriate here.

1.4. References

AL-'ADAMI, KH.

1967 Old Babylonian letters from ed-Der. *Sumer* 23-151-165, plates 1-17.

ADAMS, R. McC.

1969 Survey of ancient watercourses and settlements in central Iraq. *Sumer* 14: 101-103, figures 1-6.

1972 Settlement and irrigation patterns in ancient Akkad. Appendix 5, pp. 182-208. In *The city and area of Kish* by M. Gibson. Field Research Projects, Coconut Grove, Miami.

BORGER, R.

1958 Einige altbabylonische Koenigsinschriften aus Kiš. *Orientalia N.S.* 27:407-408.

1967 *Handbuch der Keilschriftliteratur*, vol. 1: Repertorium der sumerischen und akkadischen Texte. Walter de Gryter, Berlin.

CHARPIN, D.

1978a Recherches sur la "dynastie de Manana:" essai de localisation et de chronologie. *Revue d'assyriologie* 72:13-40.

1978b Nouveaux textes de la "dynastie de Manana." *Revue d'assyriologie* 72:139-150.

1979 Review of S. Simmons, *Early Old Babylonian documents. Bibliotheca Orientalis* 36:188-200.

DALLEY S.

1979 *A catalogue of the Akkadian cuneiform tablets in the collections of the Royal Scottish Museum, Edinburgh, with copies of the texts.* Information series of the Royal Scottish Museum, Art and Archaeology 2, Edinburgh.

VAN DIJK, J. J.

1968 *Old Babylonian texts and related materials.* Texts in the Iraq Museum, vol. 6. Otto Harrassowitz, Wiesbaden.

EDZARD, D. O.

1957 *Die "zweite Zwischenzeit" Babyloniens.* Otto Harrassowitz, Wiesbaden.

1970 *Altbabylonische Rechts- und Wirtschaftsurkunden aus Tell ed-Dēr im Iraq Museum, Baghdad.* Verlag der Bayerischen Akademie der Wissenschaften, Munich.

EDZARD, D. O. (cont.)

1976 Ilip. Entry in *Reallexikon der Assyriologie*, vol. 5, 1/2:52. D. O. Edzard, ed. Walter de Gruyter, Berlin.

EDZARD, D. O. and G. FARBER

1974 *Die Orts- und Gewaessernamen der Zeit der 3. Dynastie von Ur*. Répertoire géographique des textes cunéiformes, vol. 2. Dr. Ludwig Reichert Verlag, Wiesbaden.

FALKENSTEIN, A.

1963 Zu den Inschriftenfund der Grabung in Uruk-Warka 1960-61. *Baghdader Mitteilungen* 2:1-82.

FINKELSTEIN, J. J.

1955 Subartu and Subarians in Old Babylonian sources. *Journal of Cuneiform Studies* 9:1-7.

1966 The genealogy of the Hammurapi dynasty. *Journal of Cuneiform Studies* 19:95-118.

1972 *Late Old Babylonian documents and letters*. Yale Oriental Series, Babylonian Texts, vol. 13. Yale University Press, New Haven.

FISH, T.

1952a New Ammiditana texts. *Manchester Cuneiform Studies* 2:38-43.

1952b New Ammizaduqa texts. *Manchester Cuneiform Studies* 2:27-30.

GELB, I. J.

1961 Review of D. O. Edzard, *Die "zweite Zwischenzeit" Babyloniens*. *Journal of Near Eastern Studies* 20:266-270.

1977 Thoughts about Ibla: a preliminary evaluation, March 1977. *Syro-Mesopotamian Studies* 1/1:3-20.

DE GENOUILLAC, H.

1924 *Premières recherches archéologiques à Kich: mission d'Henri de Genouillac 1911-1912*, vol. 1: Rapport sur les travaux et inventaires, fac-similés, dessin, photographies et plans. Librairie ancienne Edouard Champion, Paris.

1925 *PRAK* 2, vol. 2: Notes archéologiques et inventaires, fac-similés, dessins et photographies. Librairie ancienne Edouard Champion, Paris.

GIBSON, M.

1972a *The city and area of Kish*. Field Research Projects, Coconut Grove, Miami.

1972b The archaeological uses of cuneiform documents: patterns of occupation at the city of Kish. *Iraq* 34:113-123.

GOETZE, A.

1950 Sumu-yamūtbāl, a local ruler of the Old-Babylonian period. *Journal of Cuneiform Studies* 4:65-72.

GORDON, C.

1952 *Smith College tablets: 110 Cuneiform texts selected from the college collection*. Department of History of Smith College, Northampton, Massachusetts.

GRANT, E.

1938 Ten Old Babylonian contracts. In *The Haverford symposium on archaeology and the Bible*, ed. E. Grant, pp. 225-245. American Schools of Oriental Research, New Haven.

GRAYSON, A. K. and E. SOLLBERGER

1976 L'insurrection générale contre Naram-Suen. *Revue d'assyriologie* 70:103-128.

GREENGUS, S.

1979 *Old Babylonian tablets from Ishchali and vicinity*. Nederlands Historisch-Archaeologisch Instituut te Istanbul.

HORSNELL, M.

1974 *The year-names of the First Dynasty of Babylon: with a catalogue of the year-names from Sumuabum to Samsuiluna*. Unpublished Ph.D. dissertation, University of Toronto.

HUNTER, G. R.

1930 *Sumerian contracts from Nippur*. Oxford Editions of Cuneiform Texts, vol. 8. Oxford University Press, Oxford.

JACOBSEN, T.

1940 Historical data; the succession of the rulers in Eshnunna during the second half of the Larsa period. In *The Gimilsin temple and the palace of the rulers at Tell Asmar*, H. Frankfort, S. Lloyd and T. Jacobsen, pp. 116-131. Oriental Institute Publications, vol. 43. University of Chicago Press, Chicago.

1960 The waters of Ur. *Iraq* 22:174-185.

JOHNS, C. H. W.

1910 Babylon. *Proceedings of the Society of Biblical Archaeology* 32:272-282.

1911 The Manana-Iapium dynasty at Kish. *Proceedings of the Society of Biblical Archaeology* 33:98-103.

1914 Some Babylonian tablets in the Manchester Museum. *Journal of the Manchester Egyptian and Oriental Society* 3:67-72.

KIENAST, B.

1978 *Die altbabylonischen Briefe und Urkunden aus Kisurra*. 2 vols. Franz Steiner Verlag, Wiesbaden.

KLENGEL, H.

1971 Drei altbabylonische Urkunden betreffend Felder von *ugbabtum*-Priesterinnen. *Journal of Cuneiform Studies* 23:124-129.

1973 *Altbabylonische Rechts- und Wirtschaftsurkunden*. Vorderasiatische Schriftdenkmaeler der Staatlichen Museen zu Berlin, vol. 18. Akademie Verlag, Berlin.

KRAUS, F. R.

1952-53 Kazallu und andere nordbabylonische Kleinstaaten vor der Zeit des Hammurabi. *Archiv fuer Orientforschung* 16:319-322.

KRAUS, F. R. (cont.)

1955 Provinzen der neusumerischen Reiches von Ur. *Zeitschrift fuer Assyriologie* 51:45-75.

1972 *Briefe aus dem Istanbuler Museum*. Altbabylonische Briefe in Umschrift und Uebersetzung, vol. 5. E. J. Brill, Leiden.

KUPPER, J. R.

1957 *Les nomades en Mésopotamie au temps des rois de Mari*. Société d'Edition "Les belles lettres", Paris.

1959 Lettres de Kiš. *Revue d'assyriologie* 53:19-38; 177-182.

LANGDON, S.

1911 Tablets from Kiš. *Proceedings of the Society of Biblical Archaeology* 33: 185-196; 232-242.

1924 *Excavations at Kish*, vol. 1. Librairie Orientaliste Paul Geuthner, Paris.

1927 Tablets found in Mound Z at Harsagkalamma (Kish) by the Herbert Weld (for Oxford) and Field Museum Expedition. *Revue d'assyriologie* 24:89-98.

LEEMANS, W. F.

1960 *Legal and administrative documents of the time of Hammurabi and Samsuiluna (mainly from Lagaba)*, Studia ad tabulas cuneiformes collectas a F. M. Th. de Liagre Boehl pertinentia SLB I (3). E. J. Brill, Leiden.

1966 King Alumbiumu. *Journal of Cuneiform Studies* 20:48-49.

LUTZ, H. F.

1932 Real estate transactions from Kish. *University of California Publications in Semitic Philology* 10/3:187-216.

MICHALOWSKI, P.

1978 Review of S. N. Kramer and O. Gurney, *Sumerian literary texts in the Ashmolean Museum*. *Journal of Near Eastern Studies* 37:343-345.

MOOREY, P. R. S.

1966 A reconsideration of the excavations on Tell Ingharra (East Kish), 1923-1933. *Iraq* 28:18-51.

1978 *Kish Excavations 1923-33*. Clarendon, Press, Oxford.

NIES, J. and C. KEISER

1920 *Historical, religious and economic texts and antiquities*. Babylonian Inscriptions in the Collection of James B. Nies, vol. 2. Yale University Press, New Haven.

POMPONIO, F.

1976 La "dinastia" di Mananâ. *Oriens Antiquus* 15:277-294.

REINER, E.

1961 The year dates of Sumu-jamutbal. *Journal of Cuneiform Studies* 15:121-124.

RENGER, J.

1970 Zur Lokalisierung von Karkar. *Archiv fuer Orientforschung* 23:73-78.

RIFTIN, A.

1937 *Starovavilonskie juridičeskie i administrativnie documenti v sobranijach SSSR*. Moscow.

RUTTEN, M.

1958-60 Un lot de tablettes de Manana. *Revue d'assyriologie* 52:(1958)208-225; 53:(1959)77-96; 54:(1960)19-40; 147-152.

SIMMONS, S.

1960-61 Early Old Babylonian tablets from Harmal and elsewhere. *Journal of Cuneiform Studies* 14:(1960)75-87; 117-125; 15:(1961)49-58; 81-83.

1978 *Early Old Babylonian documents*. Yale Oriental Series, Babylonian Texts, vol. 14. Yale University Press, New Haven.

SJÖBERG, A. and E. BERGMANN

1969 *The collection of Sumerian temple hymns*. Texts from Cuneiform Sources, vol. 3. J. J. Augustin, Locust Valley, New York.

SOLLBERGER, E.

1969 Samsu-iluna's bilingual inscriptions C and D. *Revue d'assyriologie* 63:29-43.

SPELEERS, L.

1925 *Recueil des inscriptions de l'Asie anterieure des Musées Royaux du Cinquantenaire à Bruxelles: textes sumeriens, babyloniens et assyriens*. Vanderpoorten and Companie, Bruxelles.

STOL, M.

1973 Review of J. J. Finkelstein, *Late Old Babylonian documents and letters. Journal of Cuneivorm Studies* 25:215-233.

1976 *Studies in Old Babylonian History*. Nederlands Historisch-Archaeologisch Instituut te Istanbul.

SZLECHTER, E.

1963 *Tablettes juridiques et administratives de la IIIe dynastie d'Ur et de la Ire dynastie de Babylone conservées au Musée de l'Université de Manchester et, à Cambridge, au Musée Fitzwilliam, à l'Institut d'Etudes Orientales et à l'Institut d'Egyptologie*. Tome I, planches; tome II, transcriptions-traductions-commentaire. Recueil Sirey, Paris.

THUREAU-DANGIN, F.

1909 L'Emplacement de Kis. *Orientalistische Literaturzeitung*: 205-207.

1911 Ašduni-erim roi de Kiš. *Revue d'assyriologie* 8:65-79.

VEENHOF, K.

1973 An Old Babylonian deed of purchase of land in the de Liagre Boehl collection. In *Symbolae Biblicae et Mesopotamicae Francisco Mario Theodoro de Liagre Boehl Dedicatae*, A. A. Kampman, ed., pp. 359-379. E. J. Brill, Leiden.

WALTERS, S.

1973 The year-names of Sumu'el. *Revue d'assyriologie* 67-21-40.

YOFFEE, N.

1977a *The economic role of the crown in the Old Babylonian period.* Bibliotheca Mesopotamica, vol. 5. Undena Publications, Malibu.

1977b The Old Babylonian texts from Kish: a first report. In *Ancient Near Eastern studies in memory of J. J. Finkelstein*, M. de J. Ellis, J. Cooper, and N. Yoffee, eds., pp. 219-223. Memoirs of the Connecticut Academy of the Arts and Sciences, Archon Books, Hamden.

1977c Kings of Marad in the Old Babylonian period. Paper delivered at the annual meeting of the American Oriental Society, Ithaca, April 1977 (abstract published).

1978 On studying Old Babylonian history. *Journal of Cuneiform Studies* 30: 18-32.

CHAPTER 2

TEXT CATALOGUES

2.1. Register of Texts Copied

Ki	Figure no.	Plate no.	*PRAK* A/B no.	*PRAK* Plate no.	Contents and date
46	1		A 46	not copied	Account of grain rations
73	1		A 73	not copied	Unaddressed letter
78	1		A 78	not copied	Allotment of *pīhu*; Samsu᾿iluna 3 or 4
591	1		B 1	not copied	Account of monthly payments
607	2-3	II-III,	B 17	6	Marriage-adoption contract; see Ch. 4.
618	4	IV-V	B 28	not copied	Envelope preserving obv. of Ki 607; see Ch. 4
627	5		B 37	not copied	Payments to the crown; Samsu᾿iluna 5
632	5		B 42	8	Receipts of barley; date broken
645	6		B 56	10	Date only preserved, Samsu᾿iluna 5
656	6		B 67	not copied	Samsu᾿iluna 11 (?)
660	6		B 71	10	Flocks of PN; Abi᾿ešuh "y"
661	7		B 72	10	Sinmuballiṭ 1 (cf. Stol 1976:28)
667	7		B 77	not copied	House rental
672	7		B 84	11	Order to give silver for harvesters to the 'lady of Kish'; Samsu᾿iluna (?)
729	8		B 141	15	Report concerning grain
730	8		B 142	15	See Ch. 3; Sinmuballiṭ 11
733	9		B 145	not copied	Fragment of letter (?)
738	9		B 151	not copied	Grain account; date incomplete
767	9		B 180	17	Date preserved; Samsu᾿iluna 6
789	9		B 203	18	Date only preserved; Sumula᾿el 5
808	10		B 223	18	List of troops/workers; Sumula᾿el 32
845	11		B 262	21	Administrative account; Sumula᾿el 33
863	12		B 280	not copied	Hammurabi 16

Ki	Figure no.	Plate no.	*PRAK* A/B no.	*PRAK* Plate no.	Contents and Date
878	12		B 295	22	Expenditure of silver to *bārû*
883	12		B 300	not copied	Delivery of flour; Apilsin 8 (or Abi'ešuh "r")
884	13		B 301	23	Report on silver, cloaks brought to Kish; Hammurabi 15
922	13		B 349	not copied	Grain for workers
946	14		B 363	not copied	Hammurabi 14 (in text)
960	14		B 377	not copied	See Ch. 3; Sinmuballiṭ 11
971	15		B 388	not copied	Allotments of grain
984	16		B 401	not copied	See Ch. 3; Sinmuballiṭ 11
990	16		B 407	not copied	See Ch. 3; Sinmuballiṭ 11
991	17		B 408	not copied	See Ch. 3; Sinmuballiṭ 11
999	17		B 416	29	Basket label of storehouse; date unplaced
1002	18		B 419	not copied	See Ch. 3; Sinmuballiṭ 11
1009	18		B 423	not copied	Date only preserved; mu é ^{d}inanna KI.BAL.MAŠ.DÀ
1017	19	I	B 428	not copied	See Ch. 3; Sinmuballiṭ 11
1023	19		B 432	not copied	See Ch. 3; Sinmuballiṭ 11
1024	20		B 433	not copied	Broken document concerning slaves; Samsu'iluna 1(?)
1027	20		B 436	32	Disbursements; Hammurabi 14
1034	21		B 443	not copied	Broken contract
1036	21		B 445	not copied	Promissory note for reeds; Sinmuballiṭ 8
1040	22		B 449	not copied	See Ch. 3; Sinmuballiṭ 11
1041	22		B 450	not copied	See Ch. 3; Sinmuballiṭ 11
1056	23-24	VI	B 466	not copied	Rations by household; see Ch. 5

(Note: Dimensions of texts are given in *PRAK* catalogues)

2.2. Register of Dated Texts

Text	Date	*PRAK* vol. and pl. no.	Figure no.	Plate no.
D 49 (Drehem?)	Šulgi 39	2, 47		
D 6	Sumuditan	2, 30		
Ki 789 (B 203)	Sumula'el 5	1, 18	9	
C 76	Sumula'el 27	2, 14		
Ki 808 (B 223)	Sumula'el 32	1, 18	10	
Ki 845 (B 262)	Sumula'el 33	1, 21	11	
D 35	Sabium 11	2, 41		
C 37	Apilsin 8	2, 8		
Ki 883 (B 300)	Apilsin 8	not copied	12	
Ki 1009		not copied	18	

Text	Date	*PRAK* vol. and pl. no.	Figure no.	Plate no.
Ki 661 (B 72)	Sinmuballiṭ 1	1, 10	7	
C 67	Sinmuballiṭ 1	2, 13		
D 27	Sinmuballiṭ 8	2, 38		
Ki 1036 (B 445)	Sinmuballiṭ 8	not copied	21	
Ki 730 (B 142)	Sinmuballiṭ 11	1, 15	8	
Ki 960 (B 377)	Sinmuballiṭ 11	not copied	14	
Ki 984 (B 401)	Sinmuballiṭ 11	not copied	16	
Ki 990 (B 407)	Sinmuballiṭ 11	not copied	16	
Ki 991 (B 408)	Sinmuballiṭ 11	not copied	17	
Ki 1002 (B 419)	Sinmuballiṭ 11	not copied	18	
Ki 1017 (B 428)	Sinmuballiṭ 11	not copied	19	I
Ki 1023 (B 432)	Sinmuballiṭ 11	not copied	19	
Ki 1040 (B 449)	Sinmuballiṭ 11	not copied	22	
Ki 1041 (B 450)	Sinmuballiṭ 11	not copied	22	
C 40	Sinmuballiṭ 11	2, 9		
C 43	Sinmuballiṭ 11	2, 9		
C 44	Sinmuballiṭ 11	2, 9		
C 104	Sinmuballiṭ 11	2, 20		
D 26	Sinmuballiṭ 11	2, 38		
D 36	Sinmuballiṭ 11	2, 41		
D 14	Hammurabi 14	2, 33		
Ki 1027 (B 436)	Hammurabi 14	1, 32	20	
Ki 946 (B 363)	Hammurabi 14	not copied	14	
C 29	Hammurabi 15	2, 7		
Ki 884 (B 301)	Hammurabi 15	1, 23	13	
C 123	Hammurabi 15	2, 24		
Ki 863 (B 280)	Hammurabi 16	not copied	12	
C 85	Hammurabi 25	2, 16		
D 42	Hammurabi 26	2, 45		
C 75	Hammurabi 38	2, 14		
Ki 672 (B 84)	Samsuʾiluna	1, 11	7	
Ki 1024 (B 433)	Samsuʾiluna 1 (?)	not copied	20	
Ki 78 (A 78)	Samsuʾiluna 3 or 4	not copied	1	
C 88	Samsuʾiluna 5	2, 17		
Ki 645 (B 56)	Samsuʾiluna 5	1, 10	6	
Ki 627 (B 37)	Samsuʾiluna 5	not copied	5	
Ki 767 (B 180)	Samsuʾiluna 6	1, 17	9	
Ki 786 (B 200)	Samsuʾiluna 7	1, 18		
C 84	Samsuʾiluna 7	2, 16		
Ki 656 (B 67)	Samsuʾiluna 11 (?)	not copied	6	
D 13	Samsuʾiluna 18	2, 33		
Ki 718 (B 130)	Samsuʾiluna 18	1, 14		
D 25	Samsuʾiluna 38	2, 38		
C 73	Abiʾešuh "m"	2, 14		
Ki 660 (B 71)	Abiʾešuh "y"	1, 10	6	
C 78	incomplete	2, 15		
C 87	incomplete	2, 16		
D 44	incomplete	2, 46		
Ki 673 (B 85)	destroyed	not copied		
Ki 728 (B 140)	incomplete	1, 15		
Ki 1009 (B223)	unplaced	not copied	18	

CHAPTER 3

A BUREAU OF BRICK-PRODUCTION IN KISH DURING THE TIME OF SINMUBALLIṬ

The sixteen texts that comprise this "archive" include ten tablets conserved in Istanbul and six in Paris. While the Paris texts were all published in *PRAK* 2, de Genouillac copied only one of the tablets in Istanbul. The only published notice of these interesting documents (known to us) has been taken by Kupper in his study of Kish letters in Paris and only then because persons of authority mentioned in those letters are also officials in these texts. In fact, owing to their very partial publication, the unsatisfactory descriptions given in the *PRAK* catalogues, and occasional problems in the published copies, the importance of this group of texts has been unduly obscured.

The tablets themselves are very small—30 mm x 30 mm are about the average dimensions, approximately the size of a large postage stamp—but can contain up to a dozen crowded and cursorily impressed lines. All the texts date to the month of Abum (NE.NE.GAR), cf. van Dijk 1967:250, n. 63 for reading) in the eleventh year-name of king Sinmuballiṭ of Babylon (cf. Renger 1970:75). The ninth through twenty-seventh days of that month are recorded although a few days in the span are not attested. Since all the texts concern tasks pertaining to the production and consignment of bricks and depict an official hierarchical structure concerned with the management of these tasks and of the labor-force that performed the tasks, we have interpreted these tablets as records of a "bureau of brick-production" in Kish.

A full study of how bricks were made in Kish and for what purposes they were produced cannot be undertaken on the basis of these documents. Indeed, many of the activities essential for the production of bricks are not mentioned at all in these surviving records. By referring to a "bureau" of brick-production, therefore, we mean to describe the set of formal, administrative procedures that are delineated in these texts, not the entire range of activities that must have been associated with brick-making in Kish. Even with this important qualification we believe the term "bureau" to be warranted and the information gleaned from the bureau's activities to be significant in the understanding of the socio-economic institutions at Kish during the time of Sinmuballiṭ.

Table 3. Brick-production Texts

Museum/text no.	Day in Abum	No. of text in Ch. 3	Figure no.	Plate no.
Ki 730	23	9	8	
960	13, 14, 15	3	14	
984	20	7	16	
990	26	12	16	
991	27	13	17	
1002	21	8	18	
1017	19	6	19	I
1023	lost	15	19	
1040	lost	16	22	
1041	lost	14	22	
C 40	24	10	*PRAK* 2 9	
C 43	9	1	9	
C 44	24	11	9	
C 104	14	2	20	
D 26	14-17	4	38	
D 36	18	5	41	

3.1. Transliterations and Translations

1. day 9 (C 43)

obv.	14 lú-hun-gá-meš	14 salaried, hired workers
	ša kù-babbar-*im*	for the purpose of molding bricks.
	a-na sig$_4$ *la-ba-nim*	*waklum*-supervisors:
	ugula ^{d}*za-ba$_4$-ba$_4$-ìl*	Zababa'il and Nuršamaš
	ù nu-úr-^{d}utu	
rev.	iti NE.NE.GAR ud 9-kam	
	[mu] bàd IM^{ki}	
seals	^{d}*za-ba$_4$-ba$_4$-ìl*	
	dumu *ig-mi-il*	
	nu-úr-^{d}utu	
	dumu ^{d}utu-ma-an-sum	

2. day 14 (C 104)

obv.	18 lú-hun-gá-meš	18 salaried, hired workers
	ša kù-babbar *a-na al-tar-ri*	for the purpose of doing *altarum*-work
	níg-šu ^{d}EN.ZU-*na-di-in-šu-mi*	authority of Sinnadinšumi
	18 lú-meš	18 men, assignment by Marduknaṣir;
	šu-zu-ub-ti ^{d}AMAR.UD-*na-ṣir*	*waklum*-supervisors:
		Zababa'il and Sagilzimu.

rev.	ugula ^{d}*za-ba$_4$-ba$_4$-ìl*	
	ù sag-íl-zi-mu	
	iti NE.NE.GAR ud 14-kam	
	mu bàd IM^{ki} mu-⸢un-dù⸣	

3. days 13, 14, 15 (Ki 960)

obv.	2 lú-hun-gá-meš	2 hired workers, 13th of Abum
	iti NE.NE.GAR ⸢ud 13-kam⸣	4 hired workers, 14th of Abum
	4 lu-hun-gá-meš	6 hired workers, 15th of Abum
	iti NE.NE.GAR ud ⸢14⸣-kam	*waklum*-supervisor: Maruyatum
rev.	6 lú-hun-⸢gá-meš⸣	
	ugula *ma-ru-ya-tum*	
	iti NE.NE.GAR ud ⸢15-kam⸣	
	mu bàd IM^{ki}	
seal	[^{d}AMAR.UD-*na-ṣ*] *i-ir*	
	dumu *ab-*[*di*]*-ìl*	
	arad$_2$ [^{d}*na*]*-bi-um*	

4. days 14, 15, 16, 17 (D 26)

obv.	1 lú-hun-gá	1 hired worker, 14th of Abum
	iti NE.NE.GAR ud 14-kam	1 hired worker, 15th of Abum
	1 lú-hun-gá-meš(sic)	2 hired workers, 16th of Abum
	iti NE.NE.GAR ud 15-kam	3 hired workers, 17th of Abum
	2 lú-hun-gá-meš	
	iti NE.NE.GAR ud 16-kam	(total) 7 hired workers
rev.	3 lú-hun-gá-meš	*waklum*-supervisor: Sagilzimu
	iti NE.NE.GAR ud 17-kam	
	7 lú-hun-gá-meš	
	ugula sag-íl-zi-mu	
	iti NE.NE.GAR ud 17-kam	
	mu bàd IM^{ki} mu-un-dù	

5. day 18 (D 36)

obv.	4 lú-hun-gá-meš kù-babbar	4 salaried, hired workers
	níg-<šu> ^{d}EN.ZU-*na-di-*⸢in⸣*-šu-mi-i*[*m*]	authority of Sinnadinšumim
	a-<*na*> *na-al-ba-nim*	for the purpose of brick-molding.
	ugula *ma-ru-ya-tum*	*waklum*-supervisor: Maruyatum
rev.	iti NE.NE.[GAR]	
	[ud] 18-kạm	
	[mu] bàd IM^{ki}	

6. day 19 (Ki 1017)

obv. 4 lú-hun-gá-meš
ša kù-babbar-*im*
a-na sig$_4$-hi-a *la-ba-nim*
ugula *ma-ru-ya-tum*

rev. níg-šu ^{d}EN.ZU-*na-di-in-šu-mi-im*
iti NE.NE.GAR ud 19-kam
mu bàd IM^{ki}

seal ^{d}AMAR.UD-*na-ṣi-ir*
dumu *ab-di-ìl*
arad$_2$ ^{d}*na-bi-um*

4 salaried, hired workers
for the purpose of molding bricks
waklum-supervisor: Maruyatum
Authority of Sinnadinšumim

7. day 20 (Ki 984)

obv. 4 lú-hun-gá-meš kù-babbar
a-na sig$_4$-hi-a
la-ba-nim
níg-šu ^{d}EN.ZU-*na-di-in-šu-mi*

lower edge
ugula *ma-ru-ya-tum*

rev. iti NE.NE.GAR ud-20-kam
mu bàd IM^{ki}

seal ^{d}AMAR.UD- [*na-ṣi-*]*ir*
dumu *ab-di-ìl*
arad$_2$ ^{d}*na-bi-um*

4 salaried, hired workers
for the purpose of molding bricks;
Authority of Sinnadinšumi
waklum-supervisor: Maruyatum

8. day 21 (Ki 1002)

obv. 25 lú-meš
šu-zu-ub-ti ^{d}AMAR.UD-*na-*⸢*ṣir*⸣
ugula ^{d}EN.ZU-*ma-gir*

rev. iti NE.NE.GAR ud 21-kam
mu bàd IM^{ki} mu-dù

25 men
assignment by Marduknaṣir
waklum-supervisor: Sinmagir

9. day 23 (KI 730)

obv. 12 lú-hun-gá-meš
ša kù-babbar-*im*
a-na sig$_4$ *za-ba-lim*
níg-šu *še-rum-ì-lí*

lower edge
45(?) aga-uš-meš
šu-zu-ub-tum

12 salaried, hired workers
for the purpose of hauling bricks;
Authority of Šerumili.
45(?) *rēdû*-soldiers
assignment by Marduknaṣir.
waklum-supervisors:
Nuršamaš and Zababa'il

rev.	[^{d}AM] AR.UD-*na-ṣir*	
	[ugula *nu-úr*]-^{d}utu	
	[*ù* ^{d}*z*]*a-ba*$_4$-*ba*$_4$-*ìl*	
	[iti NE.] NE.GAR	
	[ud] 23-kam	
	[mu] bàd IM^{ki}	

10. day 24 (C 40)

obv.	11 lú-meš	11 men
	šu-zu-ub-ti ^{d}AMAR.UD-*na-ṣir*	assignment by Marduknaṣir
	a-na ^{d}EN.ZU-*ma-gir*	to (the supervision of) Sinmagir
rev.	iti NE.NE.GAR ud 24-kam	
	mu bàd IM^{ki} mu-dù	

11. day 24 (C 44)

obv.	8 lú-hun-gá-meš	8 salaried, hired workers
	ša kù-babbar-*im*	for the purposes of doing *altarum*-work ;
	a-na al-ta-ri-im	authority of Šerumili
	níg-šu *še-rum-ì-lí*	*waklum*-supervisors:
		Nuršamaš and Zababa'il
rev.	ugula *nu-úr*-^{d}utu	
	ù ^{d}*za-ba*$_4$-*ba*$_4$-*ìl*	
	iti NE.NE.GAR	
	ud 24-kam	
	[m]u bàd IM^{ki}	

12. day 26 (Ki 990)

obv.	10 lú-meš	10 men
	šu-zu-ub-ti ^{d}AMAR.UD-*na-ṣir*	assignment by Marduknaṣir
	ugula ^{d}EN.ZU-*ma-gir*	*waklum*-supervisor: Sinmagir
rev.	iti NE.NE.GAR ud 26-kam	
	mu bàd IM^{ki}	

13. day 27 (Ki 991)

obv.	6 lú-hun-gá-<meš>	6 salaried, hired workers
	ša kù-babbar-*im*	for the purpose of doing *altarum*-work
	a-na al-ta-ri-im	authority of Šerumili
	níg-šu *še-rum-ì-lí*	*waklum*-supervisors:
		Nuršamaš and Zababa'il

rev. ugula *nu-úr-*^{d}utu
ù ^{d}*za-ba*$_{4}$*-ba*$_{4}$*-ìl*
iti NE.NE.GAR
ud 27-kam
mu bàd IM^{ki}

seals *nu-*[*úr*]-^{d}utu
[dumu] ^{d}utu-ma-⌜an-sum⌝

^{d}*za-ba*$_{4}$*-ba*$_{4}$*-ìl*
dumu *ig-mi-ìl*

14. day lost (Ki 1041)

obv. 3 1/2 lú-hun-gá-<meš> kù-babbar
a-na na-al-ba-nu-um(sic)
níg-šu ^{d}EN.ZU*-na-di-in-su-mi*

rev. ugula sag-íl-zi-mu
iti NE.N[E.GAR ud x-kam]

upper edge
mu bàd IM^{ki}

3 1/2 salaried, hired workers
for the purpose of brick-molding
authority of Sinnadinšumi
waklum-supervisor: Sagilzimu

15. day lost (Ki 1023)

obv. 16 lú-[hun-gá-meš]
ša kù-babbar*-i*[*m*]
a-na al-ta-ri-im
níg-šu *še-ru-um-ì-lí*

rev. ugula *nu-úr-*^{d}utu
ù ^{d}*za-ba*$_{4}$*-ba*$_{4}$*-ìl*
iti NE.NE.GAR ud x-kam
mu b[àd IM^{ki}]

seals *nu-úr-*^{d}utu
dumu ^{d}utu-ma-an-sum

^{d}*za-ba*$_{4}$*-ba*$_{4}$*-ìl*
rest lost

16 salaried, hired workers
for the purpose of doing *altarum*-work
authority of Šerumili
waklum-supervisors:
Nuršamaš and Zababa'il

16. day lost (Ki 1040)

obv. 14 lú-⌜hun-gá⌝-meš
ša kù-babbar[*-im*]
a-na al-t[*a-ri*]*-im*
níg-šu *še-ru-*[*um*]*-ì-lí*

14 salaried, hired workers
for the purpose of doing *altarum*-work
authority of Šerumili
waklum-supervisors:
Nuršamaš and Zababa'il

rev. ugula *nu-úr*-^{d}utu
ù ^{d}*za-ba$_4$-ba$_4$-ìl*
iti NE.NE.GAR ud[x-kam]
mu bàd IM^{ki}

seals [*nu-úr*]-^{d}[utu]
[dumu ^{d}]utu-ma-an-[sum]
arad$_2$ [*na-bi-um*]

^{d}*za-ba$_4$-ba$_4$-ìl*]
dumu *ig-mi-*[*ìl*]
arad$_2$ ^{d}⌜EN⌝.ZU

Table 4. Outline of Officials and Tasks

A. Officials
  1. Highest official: Marduknaṣir
    a. In texts Ki 730, 990, 1002; C 40, 104; seals of Ki 960, 984, 1017
    b. Always following the words *šūzubtum/šūzubti*
    c. With *waklum*-supervisor Sinmagir in Ki 990, 1002; C 40
    d. With *waklum*-supervisors Zababa'il and Sagilzimu in C 104
    e. With *waklum*-supervisors Zababa'il and Nuršamaš in Ki 730
    f. With *awīlū* in Ki 990, 1002; C 40, 104; with *rēdû*-soldiers in Ki 730
    g. Never with *agrū ša kaspim* "salaried, hired men"
    h. In seals: son of Abdi'il, servant of Nabium
    i. Specific tasks never mentioned.
  2. Bureau secretaries: Šerumili and Sinnadinšumi(m)
    a. Šerumili in texts Ki 730, 991, 1023, 1040; C 44
      (1) Always following the term níg-šu
      (2) Always with *waklum*-supervisors Nuršamaš and Zababa'il
      (3) In one memo with Marduknaṣir (Ki 730)
      (4) Tasks
        (a) *ana libnātim zabālim* (Ki 730)
        (b) *ana altarim* (Ki 991, 1023, 1040; C 44)
    b. Sinnadinšumi(m) in texts Ki 984, 1017, 1041; C 104; D 36
      (1) Always following the term níg-šu
      (2) With *waklum*-supervisor Maruyatum in Ki 984, 1017; D 36
      (3) With *waklum*-supervisor Sagilzimu in Ki 1041
      (4) With *waklum*-supervisors Zababa'il and Nuršamaš in C 104; Marduknaṣir in same memo
      (5) In two memos with seal of Marduknasir Ki 984, 1017
      (6) Tasks
        (a) *ana nalbanim* (Ki 1041; D 36)
        (b) *ana libnātim labānim* (Ki 984, 1017)
        (c) *ana altarri* (C 104)
  3. *waklum*-supervisors
    a. Zababa'il and Nuršamaš together in texts Ki 730, 991, 1023, 1040; C 43, 44
      (1) Always titled ugula
      (2) Zababa'il in one text with Sagilzimu (C 104)
      (3) Under the authority of Šerumili in Ki 730, 991, 1023, 1040; C 44
      (4) Zababa'il under authority of Sinnadinšumi(m) in C 104

(5) With no superior in C 43
(6) In seals
(a) Zababa'il is son of Igmil (<Igmilil), servant of Sin
(b) Nuršamaš is son of Utumansum, servant of Nabium
(7) Tasks
(a) *ana altarim* (Ki 730, 991, 1023, 1040; C 44
(b) *ana altarri* (C 104)
(c) *ana libnātim labānim* (C 43)

b. Maruyatum in texts Ki 960, 984, 1017; D 36
(1) Always titled ugula
(2) Under the authority of Sinnadinšumi(m) in Ki 984, 1017: D 36
(3) With no superior and no specific task in Ki 960 (summary memo)
(4) In two memos with seal of Marduknaṣir (Ki 960, 984, 1017)
(5) Tasks
(a) *ana libnātim labānim* (Ki 984, 1017)
(b) *ana nalbanim* (D 36)

c. Sagilzimu in texts Ki 1041; C 104; D 26
(1) Always titled ugula
(2) Under the authority of Sinnadinšumi(m) in Ki 1041; C 104
(3) With no superior in D 26 (summary memo)
(4) Tasks
(a) *ana* nalbanum(sic) (Ki 1041)
(b) *ana altarri* (C 104)

d. Sinmagir in texts Ki 990, 1002; C 40
(1) Titled ugula in Ki 990, 1002
(2) *ana* Sinmagir in C 40
(3) Always under disposition of Marduknaṣir
(4) No specific tasks.

B. Tasks
1. *ana altarim* (with variant *altarri*)
(Ki 991, 1023, 1040; C 44, 104)
2. *ana libnātim zabālim*
(Ki 730)
3. *ana libnātim labānim*
(Ki 984, 1017; C 43)
ana nalbanim
(Ki 1041; D 36)
4. *šūzubti* Marduknaṣir
(Ki 730, 990, 1002; C 40, 104)
5. summary memos
(Ki 960; D 26)

3.2. Excursus: Letters from Kish

The only published reference to these texts concerning brick-production of which we are aware was that made by Kupper in connection with his editions of the letters recovered by de Genouillac and conserved in Paris (Kupper 1959). Kupper observed that the most important and most frequently mentioned of the correspondents, a certain Tutunišu, could be dated according to his association with personnel who were also recorded in "une serie de contrats de louage d'ouvriers" (Kupper 1959:20). Since these "contracts" were all dated with the eleventh year-name of Sinmuballiṭ he justifiably reasoned that the letters to and from Tutunišu must have been written at about that time. Kupper was further able to cite a letter to Tutunišu from Sinmuballiṭ himself which verified this chronological placement. Since Tutunišu seems to have been a provincial governor at Kish (probably with the title *šāpir mātim/šāpir Kiš*, Kupper 1959:2-22), it will be useful to examine, if briefly, the contexts of his communications with those individuals whom we have identified as officials in the "bureau of brick-production."

Marduknaṣir appears in a number of these letters–*PRAK* 2: D 32, 33, 37, 43 (cf. Kupper 1959) and in Ki 621+641, 701, 749 (cf. Kraus 1972). Although the subjects of these messages are too laconically conveyed to permit a finegrained delineation of Marduknaṣir's activities, it is clear that he functioned as a royal official. His responsibilities include accounting for various imposts and payments (D 33, D 43–funds are termed *kasap ekallim* in D 33:11), for irrigated lands (D 32), and for other provisions from the royal estates (D 37). Marduknasir additionally appears in the letter *TCL* 17, 44 (Dossin 1933) which concerns the same affair depicted in D 46, although the *PRAK* text does not mention Marduknaṣir (Kupper 1959:21 and n. 2; Ebeling 1942:34-35). Presumably D 46 reflects an early investigation into the matter which was then more fully reported in the *TCL* text. The subject is a dispute over the field of a *rēdûm*-soldier and the attached *ilkum*-responsibility on the field which fell under the jurisdiction of Marduknaṣir. The *rēdûm* (coincidentally named Sinmagir, but not the like-named *waklum*-supervisor of the brick production texts) had fled his territory and so his field was placed temporarily in the crown's trust. On appeal to the king, whose instructions Marduknaṣir was following, the field was given over to the sons of the *rēdûm* who promised to perform faithfully the *ilkum*-duties incumbent with the grant of the field.

In the letters D 33 and D 43 Marduknasir's affairs also concern Sinnadinšumi and in the latter Maruyatum appears as well, all three known from our group of texts. Since the disposition of crown money is the chief subject of D 33, and Maruyatum appears as a paymaster of sorts in D 43, it is clear that all these individuals are acting in service to the state. Another brick-production official appears in the letter Ki 596 which mentions royal affairs under the disposition of Tutunišu. To sum up, the letters of Kish provide a welcome, if not notably detailed, check on the activities of the officials of our bureau. The responsibilities of these men were clearly not delimited by matters of producing bricks. Nonetheless, as we shall observe below, there are certain connections that can be drawn between the affairs of Marduknaṣir as chief of the bureau of brick-production and some of those responsibilities depicted in his correspondence with his own superiors in Kish and Babylon.

Table 5. Outline of Terms

I. Structure of the bureau
- Chief
  - Key term: *šūzubtum*
- Secretaries
  - Key term: níg-šu
- Supervisors
  - Key term: *waklum*

II. Tasks of the bureau
- *altarum*
- *libnātim labānum*
- *nalbanum*
- *libnātim zabālum*

III. Workers in the bureau
- *agrū ša kaspim*
- *awīlū*
- *rēdū*

IV. Correlation of workers and tasks
- *rēdū* and *awīlū* ––––––––– *šūzubtum*
- *agrū ša kaspim* } *altarum*, *libnātim labānum*, *nalbanum*, *libnātim zabālum*

Table 6. Hierarchy and Responsibilities

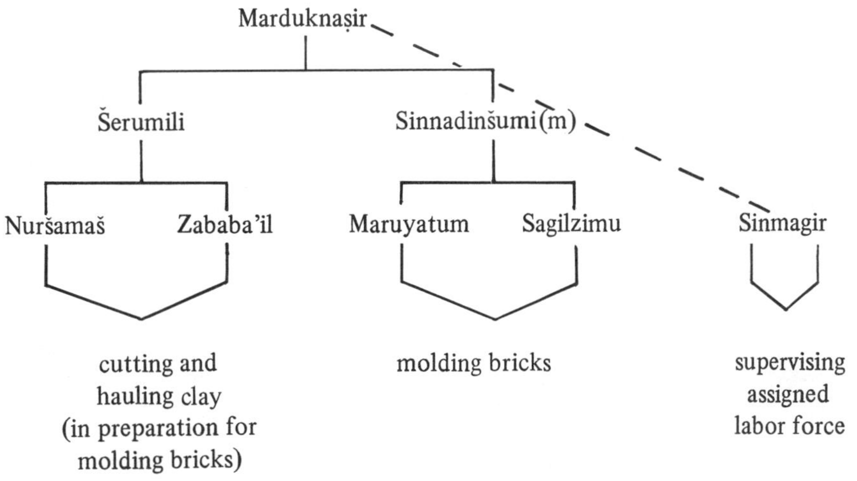

3.3. Textual Commentary

The highest official in the bureau is Marduknaṣir, and all the other officials in the sixteen texts comprising this "archive" can be shown to be under his authority. A striking example of Marduknasir's overall responsibility is seen in three texts that deal with the duties of the *waklum*-supervisor Maruyatum. Although his presence is not indicated in the texts themselves, they are all "notarized" with Marduknaṣir's seal. Apparently in his absence the authority of the head of the bureau over the activities of his subordinates could be indicated merely by the rolling of his seal on the administrative memo of his subordinate.

The function of Marduknasir in these texts is only laconically expressed, however, and much depends on the interpretation of the term *šūzubtum*. This word appears in all five texts in which Marduknasir is noted and always directly precedes his name. It is usually thus declined as the construct form *šūzubti*, although in one instance *šūzubtum* is written. In addition to the brick-production texts the term *šūzubtum/šēzubtum* occurs in Walters 1972: no. 28 (p. 32 and note 2) in a text concerning workers under the supervision of an ugula. Walters suggests a translation "safe conduct, pass", extrapolated from a meaning of *ezēbum*, but this interpretation does not seem to fit any of the other contexts in which the word is found. Goetze (1957: p. 26, no. 13, obv. line 8) compared the phase ud 3-kam *še-zu-ub-tum* in a contract dealing with the hire of workers (cf. also *YOS* 12, Feigin 1979: no. 531, lines 7-8, *i-na* iti-l ud 3-kam *šu-zu-ub-tum*) with the phrase *qātam ṣabātum*, "days off" (cf. Lautner 1936:129-133). The *CAD* (vol. Ṣ 1962, p. 30) derives the word not from *ezēbum*, but from *waṣābum*, hence *šūṣubtum*, "an added period of work" (although in vol. A/2, no Š-stem of *waṣābum* is attested). The *AHw* (1977) p. 1288, lists *šūṣubtum*, "Hinzufuegtes," on the basis of a single lexical entry. In *BA* 5/IV, no. 43, p. 508 (Friedrich 1906: cf. Schorr 1913: no. 146, pp. 206-207), lines 17-18, ud 3-kam gis-má *te-zu*!*-ub-tam i-la-ak*, also seem to indicate the "days off" of (the crew of) a boat (reference courtesy of M. Stol). In *PBS* 8/2 (Chiera 1922) no. 253, line 17, a rental of land is denoted *te-ep-ti-tum šu-zu-ub-šu*; in *AbB* 1 (Kraus 1964) no. 12, rev. 2, in a broken context in the phrase *ana šu-zu-ub-ti-ka uš-ta-bi-la-ak-kum*, Kraus has translated *šūzubtum* as "Restzahlung." The *AHw's* translation of *šūzubtum* as "eine Zahlung?" is, as the question mark indicates, no more than a guess. In *MSL* 5; 11, *šūzubtum* appears in a series—*biblu*, *šūbiltu*, *šūzubtu*.

The most common usage in the Old Babylonian period of the Š-stem of *ezēbum* is "to issue a document, issue a written order" (cf. *CAD* and *AHw, ezēbum*). Without a noun object, e.g., *ṭuppam*, *kunukkam*, the verb *šūzubum* usually implies "to issue an order," and thus the nomen actionis can be translated "an order, assignment" for this participle. This meaning of "assignment" passes simply and well in the context of the brick production archive and seems to fit also several of the other attestations of the word. Thus, *šūzubtum* may be interpreted as the "assignment" of land to be cultivated (Chiera 1922), the "assignment" of workers (Walters 1970 and all the brick-production texts). A connection between this *šūzubtum*, "assignment," and *šēzubtum/tēzubtum/šūzubtum*, "days off," which is not used in construct with personal names, seems unfounded.

The "assignment" *of* Marduknaṣir (*to* someone, cf. C 40) refers not to the "salaried, hired workers," which translation reflects the somewhat redundant phraseology of the original *agrū ša kaspim*, but rather only to the workers glossed as *awīlū* and *rēdū*. In Ki 1002, twenty-five men (*awīlū*) are designated *šūzubti* Marduknaṣir; in Ki 990, ten men are so glossed; in C 40, eleven men; in C 104, eighteen men; and in Ki 730, forty-five *rēdû*-soldiers are categorized *šūzubtum* Marduknaṣir. The brick-production texts thus exhibit a minimal pairing of workers: those who received wages and those assigned workers who probably received rations (cf. Gelb 1965). In C 104, two separate entries are recorded. In the first, eighteen *agrū ša kaspim* are noted as performing *altarum*-work, while in the second, eighteen *awīlū*, the assignment by Marduknasir, are listed. In Ki 730 a similar double-entry is found which implies that the number of workers in the two parts of C 104 is only coincidentally the same. In Ki 730, twelve *agrū ša kaspim* are initially noted along with their specific job to haul bricks, and then forty-five *rēdû*-soldiers are recorded as the *šūzubtum* of Marduknaṣir. In none of the five texts in which *šūzubtum* is employed is any specific task denoted.

(May this suggested interpretation of the term *šūzubtum* as "assignment" be compared to the name of the people denominated as *šūzubū/šūzubūtu* in the Alalah "census lists" [cf. Liverani 1975; Giakumakis, Jr. 1970:106, Dietrich and Loretz 1969:92 and n. 4.]? It has been assumed, based on the interpretation of its Hurrian counterpart ehelena, that *šūzubū* refers to individuals who were "saved" in Alalah [first stated by Speiser in 1954 but without explaining what it meant to be "saved"]. The *šūzubū*, however, occupy the second highest level in the Alalah lists, just below the *maryannu*. An interpretation "assignors" seems to pass well with the occupations of the *šūzubū* and may merit further investigation by those who study "social classes" at Alalah.)

Of the nature of the *šūzubtum*-assignment of Marduknaṣir we have at best a circumstantial set of indications. Especially important seems to be the reference to the *rēdû*-soldiers in Ki 730. It is well-known that a *rēdûm* had responsibilities of service to the crown during certain periods of the year (cf. Landsberger 1955; Evans 1962). Naturally this *ilkum*-service was under the jurisdiction of particular crown officials, and, in some measure, was bound to that portion of land the *rēdûm* received as a benefice from the crown. This is the very subject that occasioned the letters *TCL* 17, 44 (Dossin 1933) and *PRAK* 2, D 46 from Kish. In the former text Marduknaṣir is in charge of executing a decision of the king pertaining to the disposal of a field of a *rēdûm*. After the man had fled from his field and obligations, his sons petitioned the king for the land, pledging to assume the incumbent *ilkum*-duties on it. The field of a *rēdûm* was inalienable (according to paragraph 36 of the "code" of Hammurabi), because it belonged not to the man who worked it, but to the crown which bestowed it subject to certain conditions. The transfer of such a field could be arranged, however, if the new cultivator assumed the responsibilities attached to the field. In practice the "new cultivator" was often a member of the *rēdû*'s family. Marduknaṣir was one of those crown officials who was concerned with the disposition of the land of crown dependents, and, apparently, also with some of the other tasks that the *rēdûm*-dependent had to fulfill. Although we do not suggest that all the men "assigned" by Marduknaṣir were *rēdū*, we consider it likely that he was supervising a manpower pool, the members of which were required to perform certain services for the crown. Part of this source of labor could be designated for work in the bureau of brick-production.

Directly subordinate to Marduknaṣir in the hierarchy of this bureau are Šerumili and Šinnadinsumi(m). Both of these officials are qualified by the term níg-šu, "under the authority of" (cf. Yoffee 1977a:22ff), which denotes their responsibility for a particular task. The two bureau "secretaries" manage, for the most part, different activities. Also, they direct particular teams of *waklum*-supervisors who are actually charged with carrying out the work.

The *waklum*-supervisors under the authority of Šerumili are invariably Nuršamaš and Zababa'il. In four of the five texts in which he appears Šerumili administers a task denoted by the term *altarum* and in the other instance he is concerned with hauling bricks. Only one text pertaining to *altarum*-work is administered by Sinnadinšumi.

It is evident the task described *ana altarim*, "to do *altarum*-work," refers to a step in the production of bricks, but this rather rare term has not been satisfactorily explained. The dictionaries do not give a specific meaning for the word, the *CAD* simply offering "assigned work." Of the five Old Babylonian references listed by the *CAD*, three are to texts of this archive. All these citations, as well as the Ur III references in the *CAD*'s lexical entry, have to do with brick-making. In addition, the several passages cited from Sumerian literary works (*altarum* is a loan-word from Sumerian al-tar) all refer to building activities. From the "Myth of the Pickaxe" (en-e níg-du$_7$-e) a number of citations to altar-work may be adduced, perhaps the most informative of which shows that altar-work was viewed as hard labor: ur-sag ^{d}ninurta ki-bal-a al-tar-re (variant: ^{giš}al-tar-re) ba-an-gub (e.g., *UET* 6/1 26, 59 [Gadd and Kramer 1963]), "the hero Ninurta set up altar-work on the rebellious land." *YOS* 5 181, 25-26 (Grice 1919) shows that molding bricks (*libnātim epēšum*) and performing *altarum*-work (*altaram epēšum*) are complementary activities.

YOS 13 361 (Finkelstein 1972) can be added to the list of texts mentioning *altarum*. Finkelstein, apparently recalling the *altarum*-citations in the "Myth of the Pickaxe," described the text in the *YOS* 13 catalogue as a "hoeing labor contract." It will be useful to present this document in full.

YOS 13, 361

1 gín kù-babbar
a-na al-ta-ri-im
ki *a-da-al-la-lum* di-ku$_5$
^{m}*a-da-al-la-lum*
dumu *na-ka-rum*
šu ba-an-ti
u$_4$-mi i-ša-as-su-šu
al-ta-ra-am
i-il-la-ak
igi *a-wi-il-*^{d}EN.ZU dumu *e-til-pi$_4$-*^{d}⌜x⌝
igi *i-še-em-me-su-ul-la* ŠU.HA
iti gan-gan-è ud 13-kam
mu *sa-am-su-di-ta-na* lugal-e
^{d}ŠEŠ.KI en-gal-la
AN mi-ni-in-dím-ma (Samsuditana 10)
seal: ^{na_4} kišib *a-da-al-la-lum*

Adallalum son of Nakarum received 1 shekel silver for *altarum*-work from Adallalum the judge. On the day when they will summon him, he will perform the *altarum*-work.

This administrative transaction shows clearly that a "loan" of silver could be made against the promise to do *altarum*-work. The payment was received, and when the *altarum*-work was required, the judge and his personnel would summon the worker. One of the personnel, a *bā'irum*-soldier, appears in the list of witnesses. We may perhaps infer that the *bā'irum* was concerned with *altarum*-work on the same basis that accounts for the presence of *rēdû*-soldiers in Ki 730. Apparently, the obligations of crown beneficiaries for service included more than military duties, but also work on other projects on the crown's estates.

Other references to *altarum* include the docket *CT* 45 71 (Pinches 1964):

CT 45 71

1 šitim	1 builder
[x] *ša* al-tar	who did *altarum*-work
é ka-si-ga	on the shearing house.
i-pu-šu	Responsibility of Ipiqišhara.
gìr sig-^{d}*iš-ha-ra*	
(Samsu'iluna 2)	

Falkenstein (1965:299, n. 15) compares this text to Weitemeyer 1962: no. 118, in which three builders also worked under the direction of Ipiqišhara, this time on the roof (reference and reading ùr! courtesy of M. Stol) of the palace (cf. also the phrase *altaram epēšum* in the docket published by Jacobsen 1939:66). The connection of *altarum*-work with building (repairing roofs) is also indicated in Birot 1969: no. 22, lines 5-6:

Birot 1969: no. 22

40 erén-meš *ša ša-ad-da-ag-di-im*	40 troops from last year
al-ta-ra-am ša ú-ri-im i-pu-šu	who did *altarum*-work of the roof

Builders are further grouped with brick-producers in Riftin 1937: no. 53, lines 8-12:

Riftin 1937: no. 53

10 gur še lú-hun-gá-meš *ša* 1-iku sig$_4$
a-na é *a-ša-ah-ha-tim ù ka-pi-ri-im il-bi-nu*
5 gur á lú-hun-gá *ša* sig$_4$ *iz-bi-lu*
5 gur šuku lú-šitim-meš *ù* á lú-hun-gá-meš
ša é *a-ša-ah-ha-tim ù ka-pi-ra-am i-pu-šu*

10 kor grain: hired-workers who formed 1 iku-measure of bricks
for the *a*-storehouse and the *k*-building;
5 kor: wages of the hired workers who carried the bricks;
5 kor: allotment for the builders and the wages for the hired-workers
who built the *a*-storehouse and the *k*-building.

A laconic note to PN *altarum* in *VS* 9, 28:1-2 (Ungnad 1909) can be interpreted either as a profession or as an assignment. In Leemans 1966: p. 40, no. 6, lines 12 and 14, numbers of workers are glossed lú *al-ta-ru-um*, referring to fieldworkers. This reference is explained in the *CAD*'s discussion (vol. A/1, p. 374a) in which *altaru* as work is separated from lú-al-kud(-da), the one who does the work. In Greengus 1979: no. 272, lines 11-13, a summary of *altarum*-workers are credited (debited?) to a silver account:

Greengus 1979: no. 272

10 lú-hun-gá-meš
al-ta-rum
kù-babbar níg-ŠID

The precise nature of *altarum*-work is not revealed by these documents, and *altarum* is not explicated in Salonen's compendium *Die Ziegeleien im alten Mesopotamien* (1972), although Salonen does note that the element al is included in several terms that describe both implements and people employed in the brick-making process. The etymology of al-tar, presumably "to . . . with the al," (the etymology of tar is unclear) cannot be used to prove what *altarum*-work denotes. One may envision hacking the clayey-substance from a river bank or pit which would then be soaked in water and mixed with various tempers. The mixture would then be hauled to the brick-maker who would put it in the molds (cf. Salonen 1972; Speiser and Herbert 1951). References to the repair of roofs in connection with builders show that *altarum*-work also could denote cutting clay bricks for particular jobs. Since little hard information exists in the texts of this bureau (which are in fact only administrative memos) about the total number of steps necessary in the brick-making process or even the order of the tasks that are depicted in the extant records, we shall return to the investigation of the hierarchical nature of the bureau, about which the interpretations may be less provisional.

Sinnadinšumi(m—so Ki 1017) appears in five texts. In three of them he is associated with the *waklum*-supervisor Maruyatum. In four texts he is concerned with the molding of bricks, *libnātim labānum* and *nalbanum* being two different ways of saying the same thing. In the other text he administers *altarum*-work. On two tablets dealing with the responsibilities of Sinnadinšumi the seal of Marduknaṣir is rolled although Marduknaṣir takes no explicit part in the transaction. Maruyatum is the *waklum*-supervisor most often connected with Sinnadinšumi (appearing in both texts sealed by Marduknaṣir). All three of these officials may be found in the letter *PRAK* 2, D 43 which deals with payments for workers and the collection of imposts.

The *waklum*-supervisors have already been discussed in terms of their associations with the officials (bureau secretaries, as we have denominated them) under whom they serve. Nuršamaš and Zababa'il are co-workers, occurring together in six texts. Zababa'il further appears with Sagilzimu, but only in one memo. Most frequently Nuršamaš and Zababa'il oversee together *altarum*-work under the authority of Šerumili. In one text they administer the molding of bricks and in it no higher official is noted. The *waklum* Sinmagir is concerned only with the men assigned by Marduknaṣir in the three texts in which he appears. Maruyatum, when associated with a superior, as he is four times with Sinnadinšumi, oversees the molding of bricks. Sagilzimu also serves under the authority of Sinnadinšumi, once in the molding of bricks, once supervising *altarum*-work.

3.4. Summary and Implications

In summation we may say that this bureau of brick-production in Kish comprises an official hierarchy charged mainly with two specific operations: to hack the clayey-substance in preparation for molding bricks (as we provisionally interpret the task denoted by the term *altarum*) and then to mold bricks (*libnātim labānum*; *nalbanum*). Each of these two main operations was managed by a staff that specialized in that task, but there was also some overlapping. Those charged with molding bricks once supervised *altarum*-work (C 104), and the personnel primarily responsible for *altarum*-work once hauled bricks (*libnātim zabālum*, Ki 730).

The laborers actually performing the tasks supervised by the bureau fall into two categories. The first, *agrū ša kaspim*, "salaried, hired workers," were required to do specific tasks and were remunerated with silver, although silver might well have been only a standard by which commodities were disbursed (cf. Yoffee 1977a:16-18). In one text, Ki 1041, three 1/2 workers were recorded, the fraction referring obviously not to the number of men, but to the number of "man-days" to be worked. These "salaried, hired workers" presumably possessed special skills for these specific tasks.

In contradistinction to these hired specialists were the "men" and *rēdû*-soldiers who were assigned by Marduknaṣir. No particular tasks are ever recorded in connection with these workers. Evidently the labor they did required no special expertise. It seems they were summoned to work either as part of their *ilkum*-responsibilities to the crown, or as a means of repaying loans.

The socio-economic implications of this bureau's responsibilities and its hierarchical structure can best be perceived in historical perspective. As discussed in Ch. 1, after the collapse of the "Third Dynasty of Ur," Kish was singularly important among northern Babylonian cities since it symbolized a kind of political unity, similar to Nippur in the south, which was in fact lacking during this time. This significance ended, however, with the conquests of Sumulaʾel who brought together the area from Sippar in the north to Marad in the south under the administration of the previously unimportant city of Babylon. In the time of Sinmuballiṭ, third successor of Sumulaʾel, we see that the bureau of brick-production in Kish was subject to a provincial governor and ultimately to the Babylonian crown.

In fact the core area established by Sumula'el seems to have operated as a single interaction sphere with Babylon as the primary center and with other centers and their local hinterlands functioning as nodes within this network of exchange and administration. The internal dynamics depicted in this study of the bureau of brick-production at Kish illustrate in part the mechanisms by which services were mobilized in this system and the nature of the interaction between state and citizens in the period just before Hammurabi. The territory added to this stable core as a result of the remarkable conquests of Hammurabi changed the nature of bureaucratic interactions, however, and, as has been argued elsewhere (Yoffee 1977a), the new policies of overcentralization sowed the seeds of the ultimate collapse of the dynasty of Sumula'el. This harvest was amply reaped during the time of the last four kings as the crown increasingly lost control of the bureaucracy. The locally organized societal components and temple-estates correspondingly increased their own authority and wealth at the crown's expense (Yoffee 1977b). During this period of the long drawn-out decline of the centralized Babylonian government, the core area established by Sumula'el was decomposing into the locally controlled units from which it was originally put together. The Hittite raid on Babylon that formally ended the tottering Babylonian monarchy merely accentuated this process of collapse (contrast this view with Postgate 1977:100-101; echoed by Oates 1979:84).

By accumulating data on the nature of internal bureaucratic structures and their changing character, we can begin to delineate the goals and powers of the state and ultimately to frame explanations for historical change in Mesopotamia. This examination of a small archive of a bureau of brick-production at Kish offers only a glimpse into the dynamic qualities of a specialized division of labor, the information-processing network needed to coordinate various activities, and the relationship between state and non-state institutional structures during the time of Sinmuballiṭ. The texts themselves do not report on the acquisition and preparation of the raw materials that were used by the bureau, nor are all the steps essential to the production of bricks related in these sixteen memos. We are further uninformed how and for what purpose the bricks were used in construction. Each of these activities may have required a bureau of its own that entailed particular sets of skills and responsibilities. It is inherent in the nature of Mesopotamian textual data, selectively composed and differentially preserved (and published), that even the mightiest of interpretive edifices must rest on the slenderest of factual reeds.

3.5. References

BIROT, M.

1969 *Tablettes économiques et administratives d'époque babylonienne ancienne.* Paul Geuthner, Paris.

CHIERA, E.

1922 *Old Babylonian contracts.* Publications of the Babylonian Section, vol. 8, no. 2. University Museum, Philadelphia.

DIETRICH, M. and O. LORETZ

1969 Die soziale Struktur von Alalah und Ugarit (II): die sozialen Gruppen *hupše-name, hanniahhe-eku, ehele-šūzubu* und *maryanne* nach Texten aus Alalah IV. *Welt des Orients* 5:57-93.

VAN DIJK, J. J.

1967 VAT 8382: ein zweisprachiges Koenigsritual. In *Heidelberger Studien zum alten Orient*, edited by D. O. Edzard, pp. 233-268. Otto Harrassowitz, Wiesbaden.

DOSSIN, G.

1933 *Lettres de la première dynastie babylonienne.* Musée du Louvre, Département des antiquités orientales, textes cunéiformes, vol. 17. Paul Geuthner, Paris.

EBELING, E.

1942 *Altbabylonische Briefe der Louvre-Sammlung aus Larsa.* Mitteilungen der Altorientalischen Gesellschaft, vol. 15, Heft 1/2.

EVANS, G.

1962 The incidence of labour-service in the Old Babylonian period. *Journal of the American Oriental Society* 83:20-26.

FALKENSTEIN, A.

1965 Review of M. Weitemeyer (1962). *Zeitschrift fuer Assyriologie* 57:298-300.

FEIGIN, S.

1979 *Legal and administrative texts of the reign of Samsu-iluna.* Yale Oriental Series, Babylonian Texts, vol. 12. Yale University Press, New Haven.

FINKELSTEIN, J. J.

1972 *Late Old Babylonian documents and letters.* Yale Oriental Series, Babylonian Texts, vol. 13. Yale University Press, New Haven.

FRIEDRICH, T.

1906 Altbabylonische Urkunden aus Sippara. *Beitraege zur Assyriologie und semitischen Spachwissenschaft* 5/iv:413-527.

GADD, C. and S. N. KRAMER

1963 *Literary and religious texts*. Ur Excavations, texts, vol. 6, part 1. Publications of the joint expedition of the British Museum and of the University Museum, University of Pennsylvania, Philadelphia to Mesopotamia.

GELB, I. J.

1965 The ancient Mesopotamian ration system. *Journal of Near Eastern Studies* 24:230-243.

GIAKUMAKIS, Jr., G.

1970 *The Akkadian of Alalah*. Mouton, The Hague.

GOETZE, A.

1957 Old Babylonian documents from Sippar in the collection of the Catholic University of America. *Journal of Cuneiform Studies* 11:15-40.

GREENGUS, S.

1979 *Old Babylonian tablets from Ishchali and vicinity*. Nederlands Historisch Archaeologisch Instituut te Istanbul.

GRICE, E. M.

1919 *Records from Ur and Larsa dated in the Larsa dynasty*. Yale Oriental Series, Babylonian Texts, vol. 5. Yale University Press, New Haven.

JACOBSEN, T.

1939 *Cuneiform texts in the National Museum, Copenhagen, chiefly of economical contents*. E. J. Brill, London.

KRAUS, F. R.

1964 *Briefe aus dem British Museum (CT 43 and 44)*. Altbabylonische Briefe in Umschrift and Uebersetzung, vol. 1. E. J. Brill, Leiden.

1972 *Briefe aus dem Istanbuler Museum*. Altbabylonische Briefe in Umschrift und Uebersetzung, vol. 5. E. J. Brill, Leiden.

LANDSBERGER, B.

1955 Remarks on the archive of the soldier Ubarum. *Journal of Cuneiform Studies* 9:121-131.

LAUTHER, J. G.

1936 *Altbabylonische Personenmiete und Erntearbeitervertraege*. Studia et Documenta ad Iura orientis pertinentia, vol. 1, E. J. Brill, Leiden.

LEEMANS, W. F.

1966 Cuneiform texts in the collection of Dr. Ugo Sissa. *Journal of Cuneiform Studies* 20:34-47.

OATES, J.

1979 *Babylon*. Thames and Hudson, London.

PINCHES, T.

1964 *Old Babylonian business documents*. Cuneiform texts from Babylonian tablets in the British Museum, vol. 45. London.

POSTGAGE, J. N.

1977 *The first empires.* Elsevier-Phaidon, Oxford.

RENGER, J.

1970 Zur Lokalisierung von Karkar. *Archiv fuer Orientforschung* 23:73-78.

RIFTIN, A.

1937 *Starovavilonskie juridičeskie i administrativnie dokumenti v sobranijach SSR.* Moscow.

SALONEN, A.

1972 *Die Ziegeleien im alten Mesopotamien.* Annales Academiae Scientiarum Fennicae, Series B, 171. Suomalainen Tiedeakatemia, Helsinki.

SCHORR, M.

1913 *Urkunden des altbabylonischen Zivil- und Prozessrechtes.* J. C. Hinrichs'sche Buchhandlung, Leipzig.

VON SODEN, W.

1952 *Grundriss der akkadischen Grammatik.* Analecta Orientalia, vol. 33 (first edition). Pontifical Biblical Institute, Rome.

1977 *Akkadisches Handwoerterbuch.* Lieferung 14. Otto Harrassowitz, Wiesbaden.

SPEISER, E. A.

1954 Review of D. J. Wiseman, *The Alalah tablets. Journal of the American Oriental Society* 74:18-25.

SPEISER, E. A. and H. M. HERBERT

1951 Ancient Mesopotamia. *National Geographic* 99:44-105.

UNGNAD, A.

1909 *Vorderasiatische Schriftdenkmaeler der koeniglichen Museen zu Berlin*, vol. 9. J. C. Hinrichs'sche Buchhandlung, Leipzig.

WALTERS, S.

1970 *Water for Larsa: an Old Babylonian archive dealing with irrigation.* Yale Near Eastern Researches, vol. 4. Yale University Press, New Haven.

WEITEMEYER, M.

1962 *Some aspects of the hiring of workers in the Sippar region at the time of Hammurabi.* Munksgaard, Copenhagen.

YOFFEE, N.

1977a *The economic role of the crown in the Old Babylonian period.* Bibliotheca Mesopotamica, vol. 5. Undena Publications, Malibu.

1977b The Old Babylonian texts from Kish: a first report. In *Ancient Near Eastern studies in memory of J. J. Finkelstein*, edited by M. de J. Ellis, J. Cooper, and N. Yoffee, pp. 219-223. Memoirs of the Connecticut Academy of Arts and Sciences, vol. 19, Archon Books, Hamden.

CHAPTER 4

Ki 607/618: THE ADOPTION OF MALGUMLIBLUṬ AND THE MARRIAGE OF HIS PARENTS

Ki 607 was published by de Genouillac in *PRAK* 1 as text B 17. In the catalogue of that volume he described it as a "contrat de mariage" of which only the obverse was preserved ("revers presque disparu"–de Genouillac 1924: pl. 6). Ki 618, in de Genouillac's catalogue recorded as B 28, was not copied by him but was summarized as a "fragment d'enveloppe de grande contrat, achat (2/3 de mine) et adoption (nam-ibila)." Actually, Ki 618 is the envelope of Ki 607 and Ki 607 is the reverse of the tablet (it is the obverse which is almost completely lost). Ki 618, while also fragmentary, preserves a substantial part of the obverse of the text. De Genouillac did not copy two lines of the lower edge of Ki 607 and further did not attempt to decipher the very damaged left edge which contains the oath and names of witnesses. We present here a new copy of the reverse, Ki 607, on figures 2-3 (and photos on plates II-III) and the first copy of the obverse, Ki 618, on figure 4 (photos on plates IV-V).

4.1. Transliterations

Ki 618

1′ [ ]
2′ [dum] u$^{?}$ -n[i]
3′ [x] in-na-[ ]
4′ [*ma-al-g*] *u-um*^{ki}*-li-ib-lu-*[*uṭ*]
5′ [ki *hu-ut-t*] *u-pu-um* ad-da-a-n[i]
6′ [*ù bi-i*] *k-ku-lu-um* ama-a-[ni]
7′ [nam-ibila] -a-ni-šè ^{p}*gi-mil-*[*lum* in-gar$^{?}$]
8′ [nam-ibila] -a-ni-šè ^{p}*ma-a*[*l-gu-um-li-ib-lu-uṭ*]
9′ [*gi*] -⸢*mil*⸣-[*lum*] bí-[in-sar]
10′ 2 gín kù-babbar ^{p}⸢*gi-mil*⸣*-lum ù* [EŠ$_4$ .DAR-*i-bi*]
11′ *a-na hu-ut-tu-*⸢*pu*⸣*-um* ad-da-⸢a⸣-[ni]
12′ *ù bi-ik-ku-lum* ama-a-[ni]
13′ *id-di-nu*
14′ ⸢*ù* (tablet: ⸢u$_4$-kùr-šé?⸣) ŠU.⸣ GAR.TUR.LÁ.BI ^{p}*gi-mil-lum*
15′ ⸢*ù*⸣ [EŠ$_4$.DAR-*i*] -*bi* dam-a-ni
16′ *a-na ma-al-gu-um-li-ib-lu-uṭ*

17′ dumu-meš-mu nu-me-en ba-na-an-d⸢u$_{11}$-meš⸣
18′ 1/3 ma-na kù-babbar ì-lá-e-meš
19′ *ù* nam-ibila-⸢ni⸣[*ileqqe*]
20′ *ù* ŠU.GAR.TUR.L[Á.BI *ma-al-gu-um-li-ib-lu-uṭ*]
lower edge of envelope 21′ *a-na gi-mil-*[*lum* ad-da-a-ni]
22′ *ù* [EŠ$_4$.DAR-*i-bi* ama-a-ni]

seals: 1. ma-[nu?]
[x]
[x]
2. *a-ap-pa-*[ ]
dumu ^{d}nuska[ ]
arad$_2$ ^{d}PA[ ]
3. *a-bu*[-]
dumu *ip-qu-*^{d}[ ]
[ ]

Ki 607

lower edge of tablet [1/3] ⸢ma-na kù-babbar ì-lá⸣-[e-meš]
ù nam-ibila-a-ni ⸢*i*⸣-[*le-qé-e(?)*]

rev. 1′ *ù* ŠU.GAR.TUR.LÁ.BI ^{p}*ma-a*[*l-gu-um-li-ib-lu-uṭ*]
2′ *a-na gi-mil-lum* ad-da-a-ni
3′ *ù* EŠ$_4$.DAR-*i-bi* ama-a-ni
23′ 4′ ad-da-mu nu-me-en ama-mu nu-me-en
24′ 5′ ba-na-an-du$_{11}$-meš
25′ 6′ kù-babbar in-na-ab-sum-meš
26′ 7′ 10 gín kù-babbar *te-er-ha-at* ^{p}EŠ$_4$.DAR-*i-bi*
27′ 8′ ^{p}*hu-ut-tu-pu-um ù bi-ik-ku-lum* ama-a-ni
28′ 9′ *i-na qá-ti* ^{p}*gi-mi*[*l-l*]*um* [*m*]*a-ah-ru*
29′ 10′ ^{p}*gi-mil-lum a-na* EŠ$_4$.DAR-*i-bi* dam-a-ni
30′ 11′ [d]am-mu nu-me-en ba-na-an-du$_{11}$-meš
31′ 12′ [*i*]*-na* é *i-ip-pu-šu i-te-el-li*
32′ 13′ *ù* 1/2 ma-na kù-babbar i-lá-e
33′ 14′ ^{p}EŠ$_4$.DAR-*i-bi a-na gi-mil-lum* dam-a-ni
34′ 15′ dam-mu nu-me-en ba-na-an-du$_{11}$-meš
35′ 16′ *i-ha-aš-šu-ši-i-ma a-na me!-e*
36′ 17′ *i-na-ad-du-ši*

37′ 18′ ^{p}*gi-mil-lim ù* EŠ$_4$.DAR-*i-bi*
38′ 19′ *a-di hu-ut-tu-pu-um ù bi-ki-ku-lu-um*
39′ 20′ [*ba*]-*al-ṭú it-ta-na-aš-šu*-[*šu-nu-ti*]
left edge
40′ 21′ [ud-kúr-š]è lú lú-ù
41′ 22′ [nu]-⸢mu⸣-un-gi$_4$-gi$_4$-dam
42′ 23′ [mu ^{d}E]N.⸢ZU⸣ ^{d}NIN.⸢GAL$^{(?)}$⸣
43′ 24′ [*ù* ^{d}EN].⸢ZU-*mu*⸣-[*ba-lí*]-⸢*iṭ*⸣
44′ 25′ in-[pàd]-⸢dè⸣-eš
45′ 26′ igi *ma*-[ ]
46′ 27′ igi [*a*]-*ap*-[*pa*]-[*X*] AN
47′ 28′ igi *na-bi-ì*-[*li*]-*šu*
48′ 29′ igi lú-^{d}nuska
49′ 30′ [AN-*šu*?-ES$_4$?] [DAR?]
50′ 31′ igi [^{d}EN.ZU]-[x-x]
51′ 32′ dumu$^{[i\text{-}bi]}$-^{d}EŠ$_4$.[DAR?]

4.2. Translation

a. Ki 618: 1′-3′

[Malgumliblut̩ is manumitted and adopted by Huttupum his father and Bikkulum his mother].

b. Ki 618: 4′-9′

From Huttupum his father and Bikkulum his mother Gimillum adopted Malgumliblut as his heir. Gimillum inscribed Malgumliblut as his heir.

c. Ki 618: 10′-13′

Gimillum and Ištaribbi gave 2 shekels silver to Huttupum his father and Bikkulum his mother.

d. Ki 618: 14′-Ki 607: 6′(25′)

If Gimillum or his wife Ištaribbi should say to Malgumliblut̩, "you are not our (sic) son," they will pay 20 shekels silver and his inheritance [he will take away]. If Malgumliblut̩ should say to Gimillum his father or to Ištaribbi his mother, "you are not my father, you are not my mother," they will sell him (into slavery).

e. Ki 607: 7′(26′)-19′(36′)

Huttupum and Bikkulum received from Gimillum 10 shekels silver, the bride-wealth of Ištaribbi. Should Gimillum say to Ištaribbi his wife, "you are not my wife," he will forfeit the estate which he will accumulate and he will pay ½ mina silver. Should Ištaribbi say to Gimillum her husband, "you are not my husband," they will bind her and throw her in the water.

f. 607: 18′(37′)-20′(39′)

Gimillum and Ištaribbi will support Huttupum and Bikkulum as long as they will live.

Left edge Ki 607

In future none of the parties will sue the other.
They swore by Sin, Ningal, and Sinmuballiṭ
Witnesses: Ma[ ]
Appa-[ ]AN
Nabiʾilišu
Lunuska
Ilšu'ištar(?)
Sin-
Son of Ibbiʾištar(?)

No date preserved.

4.3. Notes and Interpretations

a. lines 1′-3′

These first lines (there may be more than two lines completely missing) cannot be confidently restored on the basis of the fragmentary traces of them which remain. The logic of the text dictates that these lines should refer to the adoption and/or manumission of Malgumliblut for the reasons stated below.

b. lines 4′-9′

line 4′. The name Malgumliblut is itself distinctive. Malgûm (<Malgium) is a city thought to lie on the Tigris, south of the confluence of the Diyala, and to have been of some importance in the early part of the Old Babylonian period (Edzard 1957:159-162; Wilcke and Kutscher 1978). When occurring in the theophoric position in personal names, cities often stand for the name of the god of the city (Stamm 1939:84-85). Further, the use of a city as part of a personal name (but not Akšak) not unusually denoted a slave-name, serving to indicate the birthplace of the slave (cf. Harris 1977:47). On this admittedly fragile onomastic evidence we propose that the name "long live Malgium" was given a slave brought to Kish from the east-Tigris region (as a child—see below) and later adopted by Huttupum and Bikkulum.

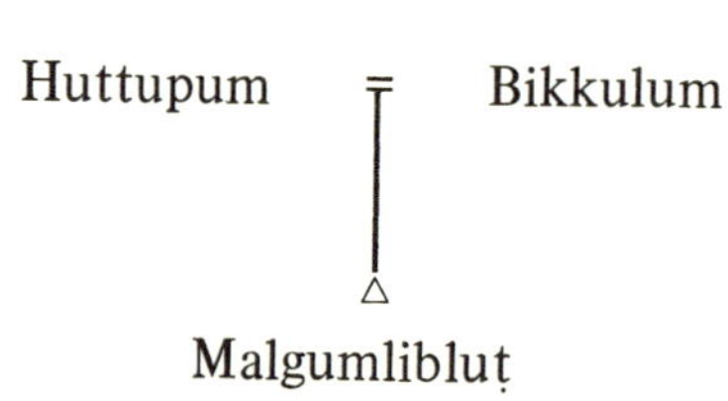

line 5′. Huttupum is likely a hypocorism for DN-uhattip, cf. *CAD* H:14g; *TLB* 4 (Frankena 1965), no. 20, line 6.

line 6′. Bikkulum (*pirrus* - formation?) is of unclear derivation; the consonants could be voiced on voiceless in the first case and voiced, voiceless, or emphatic in the second.

lines 7′-9′. In these lines it is assumed there is reference to the adoption of Malgumliblut̩ (which is required in the logic of our interpretation). The clause most commonly denoting such an action is nam-ibila-ni-šè in-gar (see, e.g., *BAP* [Meissner 1893] 97:5; *YOS* 12 [Feigin 1979] 206:7; *BE* 6/2 [Poebel 1909] 24:6). The phrase nam-dumu-ni-šè ba-da-an-ri, *e.g.*, *BE* 6/2 57:3 (here nam-dumu-ne-ne-šè) is probably excluded by the writing in our text -a-ni. Note, however, nam-ibila-ni-šè ba-an-d[a-ri], *BE* 6/2 28:3-4.

Following this declaration of adoption likely comes a reference to the official written statement. *YOS* 12 206:6-7 reads nam-ibila-ni-šè íb-ta-an-sar; cf. MSL I (Landsberger 1937:46 Tf. 3, col. iii, lines 65-66). In *CT* 8 (Pinches 1899) 49a:25-26, the phrase is *inūma* PN *ana mārtīša išṭuru*. A statement of the adoption followed immediately by its official inscription is found in *YOS* 12 206:5-7, nam-dumu-ni-šè nam-ibila-ni-šè íb-ta-an-sar.

A possible alternative reading for line 9′, assuming that herein is mentioned the marriage of Gimillum and Ištaribbi, would be [dam]-a-ni-šè ᵖ*gi-mil-*[*lum* in-du$_{12}$]. This possibility would necessitate, however, that Ištaribbi be supplied at the end of the break in line 6′ for which space seems lacking.

Since, as we learn below, Malgumliblut̩ is the son of Gimillum and receives an inheritance from him (line 19′; *aplum* must be a male, cf. Kraus 1969: 20ff; Bailey 1977), but is described initially (lines 4′-6′ and then subsequently lines 11′-12′) as the son of Huttupum and Bikkulum, it is appropriate in the intervening section for his adoption by Gimillum to be mentioned.

c. lines 10′-13′

In these lines Gimillum and Ištaribbi are seen to have given two shekels of silver to the parents of Malgumliblut̩. This amount may indicate the "fee of upbringing" (*tarbītum* = nam-á-è, or more commonly, nam-bulug$_3$) normally paid by adoptive parents to biological parents as compensation for the expenses given to a wet-nurse or otherwise are considered to have occurred in the rearing of the child. Similar fees are recorded in *BE* 6/2 4:7-8 (1 2/3 shekels) and in *UET* 5 (Figulla 1953) 92:10 (2 shekels).

d. lines 14′-25′

In this section (in which only one line requires a restoration, line 19′, see below) the relationships among the five characters in this contract is greatly clarified. Lines 14′-17′ state that Gimillum and Ištaribbi are man and wife and that Malgumliblut̩ is their son! Since Huttupum and Bikkulum were previously denoted as parents of Malgumliblut̩, it is obvious that Gimillum and Ištaribbi have adopted him. These lines record the normal clauses for the repudiation of the adoption. The inference is that Malgumliblut̩ was quite young, for the normal penalty for a child renouncing his parents is to be sold into slavery (Westbrook 1975:16). If Gimillum and Ištaribbi renounce Malgumliblut̩, the penalty is a rather stiff fine. Further, if our interpretation is correct, they may not claim that part of the estate of Huttupum and Bikkulum that belongs to Malgumliblut̩ (see below).

line 17′. dumu-meš-mu must be translated "our son," since meš obviously cannot pluralize dumu. Sumerian grammar was presumably not the forte of this contract's scribe. Meš on the end of the verb (here and elsewhere) to indicate a plural subject, however, is not an abnormal writing in this period.

line 19′. This tentative restoration [*ileqqe*] is based on a comparison with *BAP* (Meissner 1893) 97:19. The context of this document stipulates that should adoptive parents renounce their child, he shall take away a full share of the estate. Note that in *YOS* 12

206:15-19 if the adoptive father should say to his adopted son, "you are not my son," ibila-ni l-gin_7-nam é-[a-ni] ì-ba-e, "he is (still) like one (full) heir, he will divide his estate." *BAP* 97:17-19 states that if the adoptive parents try to renounce their adopted son, ha-la-šè *ki-ma* dumu-meš PN (adoptive mother) *ù* PN_2 (adoptive father) *iš-te-en i-le-qé-e-ma* [*it*$^{(?)}$-*ta*]-*aš-šu-ú*, "he will take one share (of the inheritance) like the sons of PN and PN_2 and remove it(?).

e. lines 26′-36′

It is a commonplace in studies of Mesopotamian contracts to note that information well-known to the ancient participants was often omitted (to the detriment of the modern analyst). In Ki 607-618 not only are some crucial data missing or obscure, but also the order of presentation of what is clear seems odd. Thus we read first in lines 26′-28′ that Ištaribbi is the daughter of Huttupum and Bikkulum. She seems in fact the natural daughter (or was herself manumitted) since the *terhatum* is absent in marriage documents in which the bride is a slave (Westbrook 1975:89). It thus appears that Malgumliblut̩, the adopted (and manumitted) son of Huttupum and Bikkulum is both the brother of Ištaribbi as well as her adopted son. The relationships may be illustrated as follows:

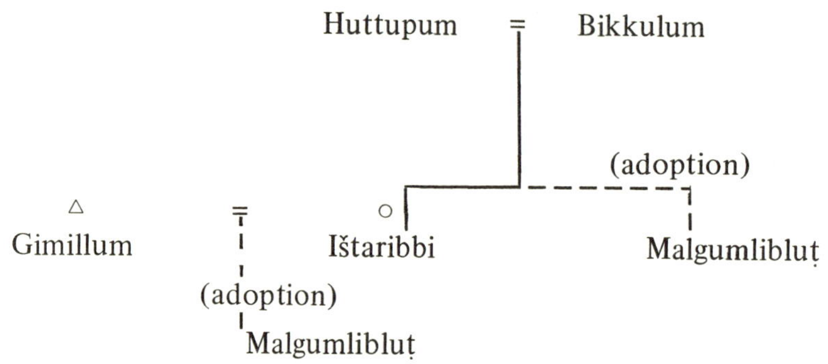

The clauses stipulating the penalities in case of divorce between Gimillum and Ištaribbi are important to the understanding of the text. Should Gimillum divorce Ištaribbi "he will forfeit the estate which he will accumulate" (a variant on the phrase *ina bītim u iniʾātim itelli*, cf. Kraus 1973:98-99, thus referring both to the immovable and movable property that composed the marital estate). The penalty, should Ištaribbi divorce Gimillum, "they shall bind her and throw her in the water," occurs in several marriage contracts (e.g., *CT* 48 [Finkelstein 1968] nos. 51, 55) and follows the forms set out in paragraph 133 of the laws of Hammurabi. Other penalties for a wife initiating divorce include that she be thrown from a parapet (*ištu dimtim*), e.g., *YOS* 12 (Feigin 1979) 371; *CT* 48 (Finkelstein 1968) 52, 56; *VS* 8 (Ungnad 1909) 4-5. In spite of these dire consequences women did divorce their husbands (cf. van Praag 1946:198; Finkelstein 1976b; Greengus 1979: no. 25), but divorce was done with ease only when the marriage was childless (cf. Westbrook 1975: Ch 4). If a woman had born children, her dowry could be contested by her husband as guardian of their children—the ultimate owners of the dowry. In *VS* 18 (Klengel 1973):114, lines 21′-23′, the phrase "if Iltani says to Ninkarak, 'you are not my husband', he will not give her daughter to her," implies that an agreement was made that whoever would initiate divorce must forfeit the offspring. In practice an action of divorce, initiated by either party, was decided on the merits of the case. Dissolution of a marriage blessed with offspring, however, had to overcome powerful deterrents (Westbrook 1975:123).

line 35′. DIŠ-E is a mistake for ME-E.

f. lines 37′-39′

Following the stipulation of the bride-wealth and divorce-clauses—and thus the declaration of the marriage of Gimillum and Ištaribbi—is the promise of that couple to support Ištaribbi's (and Malgumliblut̩'s) parents as long as they live. This support clause is found typically in contracts of manumission (see excursus below) whereby a slave is freed in return for the obligation to care for his/her aged manumittor until he/she is "summoned by his/her god." Manumission is indeed only finally effected upon the death of the manumittor when the slave has fulfilled his/her part of the contract. In this Kish text Malgumliblut is manumitted (we shall assume that Ištaribbi is the natural daughter of Huttupum and Bikkulum) and the obligation to support his adoptive parents must be his. This obligation was contractually transferred, however, to Gimillum and Ištaribbi when they adopted Malgumliblut̩ and thus assumed the legal responsibilities for the child.

Brief excursus on adoption and manumission: While there are specific words for heir and heirship, and there is a specific vocabulary for adoption, no highly regularized set of terms seems to describe the practice of manumission. For example, documents recording adoptions state that PN is the son of PN_2 or that PN_2 took PN into "sonship." In *VS* 8 (Ungnad 1909) no. 127, line 8 and *CT* 8 (Pinches 1899), no. 37d, line 9, the phrase is *ana mārūtim leqûm*; in *BAP* no. 97 (Meissner 1893), line 5, we read nam-dumu-ni-šè in-gar; in *YOS* 12 (Feigin 1979), no. 206, line 5, and in *BE* 6/2 (Poebel 1909), no. 4, lines 5-6: nam-dumu-ni-šè ba-da-an-ri; in *YOS* 12 (Feigin 1979), no. 331, line 5, *ina mêšu ana mārūtim* šu ba-an-ti; cf. David 1927 and Landsberger (*MSL* 1, 1937. Tablet 3, col. iii, lines 58 ff.).

Manumission, in contrast, involved particular rituals which usually came to stand for the act of manumission itself. In the northern part of Babylonia documents record that the slave's forehead was purified (PN sag-ki-ni in-dadag [UD.UD] = *pūssu ullil*), then turned toward the east (*ana ṣīt šamšim pānīšu iškun*). In documents from the south the technical word "freedom" might be used (ama-ar-gi$_4$ in-gar), but also the ritual of breaking an object that symbolized servitude implied manumission.

Since a number of commentators have debated just what this object was—e.g., Schorr 1913:p. 52, to line 7; Koschaker 1931:71-73; Szlechter 1952; Klíma 1964—we devote the following brief discussion of the matter. Szlechter considered that the sign in question was bi which stood for dub-bi, a tablet, indicating that a "tablet of slaveship was broken (1952:191 and n. 118). Chiera (1922:132; cf. Mendelsohn 1949:45) seems to have provided the inspiration for this interpretation, having translated the sign "tag of clay"; this was similarly followed by Klíma (1964:110). Koschaker, however, correctly read the sign as dug, "a vase," which may be now confirmed by the syllabic writing in *CT* 48 (Finkelstein 1968), 49.

CT 48, 49

1. dumu-munus *a-ra-ah-tum*
2. *kar-pa-sà ha-pi-at*
3. *qa-ab-li-it-sà ši-ib-ri-it*
4. *um-mi* aga-uš *gi-mil-*^{d}AMAR.UD
5. aga-uš *gi-mil-*^{d}AMAR.UD
6. ^{p}*a-ha-ta-ni ma-ra-sà a-di ba-al-ṭú it-ta-na-aš-ši*
7. nam dam-*šu* nam *gi-mil-*^{d}AMAR.UD *na-ad-na-at*

Arahtum is a daughter:

her vase is broken, her cup is smashed.

The mother of the *rēdû*-soldier Gimilmarduk

(the *rēdû*-soldier Gimilmarduk = dittography)

is Ahatani; her daughter will support her as long as she lives.

She (Arahtum) is given to Gimilmarduk as his wife.

This text may serve as a representative of its type (a modern study of adoption is an important desideratum of research) to be used in the interpretation of Ki 607/618. A female slave, named after the place whence she was born, the Arahtum canal (this isn't very specific; cf. Ch. 1, Map 1), was manumitted by her owner, the mother of the *rēdû*-soldier Gimilmarduk. Her manumission was symbolized by the breaking of crockery (cf. *BE* 6/2 [Poebel 1909] 8:7 also *PBS* 8/2 [Chiera 1922] 137:6). As is usual in such cases, the freed female slave was then married. Marriage represented a financial gain to the manumittor in most circumstances (cf. Westbrook 1975:15-17), but here the manumitter was simply providing a wife for her son. It is the one invariant feature of such documents for the manumission to be contingent on the freed slave supporting his/her master (in fact, it is usually the former mistress, since many such manumissions were performed by *nadītus*) in his/her old age. Since the phrase requiring such life-long support is found in Ki 607/618 we may assume that we are also dealing with a manumission in the Kish text.

Left edge.

As can be seen in the photo of the text, the left edge is very worn and difficult to reconstruct. The oath in lines 40′-44′ seems to be sworn by two deities and a king. The gods may be read Sin and Ningal, but neither of these seem to be particularly venerated in Kish or specially honored by Sinmuballiṭ. The restoration Sinmuballiṭ for the king's name is likewise very problematical. There seem to be six witnesses whose names are almost completely destroyed. The first and second witnesses are perhaps the owners of the first and second seals, respectively.

4.4. Summary

Ki 607/618, for all its many problems of interpretation, presents an interesting point of departure for the study of inheritance procedures and bilateral kinship principles. A full study of these matters, however, requires a collection and discussion of all relevant documents, which is obviously not the object of the present comments. In concluding this chapter we offer an explication of the text at hand and shall not attempt to summarize the literature on marriage, adoption, and inheritance during the Old Babylonian period. We thank R. Westbrook and E. Bailey, who have elucidated these issues in recent studies, for allowing us to cite from their works here.

It will be useful initially to sum up the respects in which Ki 607/618 *cannot* be interpreted with confidence. First is the condition of the tablet, the obverse being preserved only on the envelope and the reverse only on the tablet. Since the envelope is obviously larger than the tablet and can contain more lines of script (cf. most dramatically Finkelstein 1976a) it is regrettable that the remainder of the envelope has not turned up in Istanbul. Then, the envelope is broken at the crucial opening section when the relationships among the personae seem to be most explicitly indicated. The tablet, likewise, is severely damaged on the left edge which contains the name of the king in whose reign the tablet was written. The script seems generally datable before the time of Hammurabi, but little exactitude can be given beyond this. The language of the contract is clearly Akkadian and the Sumerian legal formulas are composed sloppily. Also, the scribe has been careless with certain signs, notably the *me* (Ki 607, line 16′), with the lack of parallelism (*Huttupum* < > *u Bikkulum* ama-a-ni, Ki 607, line 10′), the inconsistent writing of ki in the name Malgum$^{(ki)}$-liblut̩, and the sporadic use of the Personenkeil. Finally, the order of the transactions, whilst known to the participants, seems to be expressed oddly, since the marriage of Gimillum and Ištaribbi is noted only *after* their adoption of Malgumliblut̩.

If the lacunas in the text, the inelegant mode of expression, and the typically laconic statement of its main points are matters that make a full restoration of the document impossible, we may still be able to reconstruct the logic of the contract. Since Malgumliblut̩ is the central character in the proceedings, we have suggested that the first lines of the text introduced his status. Our reconstruction depends on the following arguments: First, the name Malgumliblut̩ is of a type given to slaves; next, the support clause at the end of the text implies that a manumission took place and was previously described; finally in lines 5′-6′ Huttupum and Bikkulum were stated to be the parents of Malgumliblut̩—an indication that in the preceding lines this parentage was established. From his former parents, then, Malgumliblut̩ was adopted by new parents, Gimillum and Ištaribbi. The traditional clauses state the penalties to the party who dissolves the adoption. Malgumliblut̩ seems to have been a child, since the payment of two shekels made by Gimillum and Ištaribbi to Huttupum and Bikkulum may be considered as the fee for weaning a child (or was this sum his slave-price?); then, the promise of support for a manumittor would be assumed by Gimillum and Ištaribbi if Malgumliblut̩ were too young to fulfill his obligation. The reference to the *terhatum* of Ištaribbi paid to her parents Huttupum and Bikkulum by Gimillum, if coming rather out of sequence in the text, provides the crucial facts that Ištaribbi is the daughter of Huttupum and Bikkulum and thus the (adoptive) sister of Malgumliblut̩.

Indeed, the economic advantages that accrued to every participant in this contract—and which were the reasons for its existence—depend on the pivotal role played by Ištaribbi. By marrying her, Gimillum achieved sole rights of usufruct ("the estate which he will accumulate") over the entire estate of Huttupum and Bikkulum. A husband has no claim to the property that his wife brings into the marriage as her dowry (Kraus 1969a:14-15; Bailey 1977:107 ff.) since, in time, this property would pass to their children. Bailey has emphasized that marriage-gifts can only be understood as part of inheritance procedures. Although the property brought by a wife into a marriage may normally be managed by her husband, it does not belong to him, but to their children. In Ki 607/618 the usufruct on the entire estate of Huttupum and Bikkulum was guaranteed, not only through Gimillum's marriage to their daughter, but also by her adoption of their (H + B's) adopted son. In the case of Gimillum initiating divorce, he would forfeit this property and whatever income accrued from it. Without a male heir the estate might have been contested by the brothers of Huttupum (and Bikkulum's brothers might have contested for her dowry) or their heirs (Bailey 1977:106; Kraus 1969a:9). Ištaribbi stood to inherit a part of the estate of Huttupum and Bikkulum (as a dowry—which is not mentioned in this text) and to enjoy the usufruct on that part of her parents' estate received by Malgumliblut̩.

Huttupum and Bikkulum, apparently advanced in years (as can be inferred from the support-clause) received the bride-wealth brought by Gimillum and the sum given for the upbringing of Malgumlibluṭ. More importantly, by manumitting Malgumliblut, adopting him (and thus entitling him to a share in their estate–no other children are anticipated as is sometimes the case in adoption contracts), and securing his further adoption by their daughter and her husband, they were guaranteed of material support in their old age.

The biggest beneficiary of all these complicated transactions was of course Malgumliblut. In the first place he was freed from servitude and granted a share from the estate of his adoptive parents, Huttupum and Bikkulum. As a result of being adopted by his sister, he stood to inherit her share of the estate as well. Finally, as the adopted child of Gimillum and Ištaribbi, he would also, in time, come into at least a part of his estate. The ultimate reason for undertaking all these negotiations, then, and for writing them into a single document, was to preserve the estate of Huttupum and Bikkulum in one piece and to insure the complete rights of its inheritance for Malgumliblut. By such mechanisms did one Mesopotamian family find a "loophole" in the practice of partible inheritance and a means to keep an estate intact. This loophole may have frustrated other members of the family of Huttupum and Bikkulum, but the text does not disclose so much.

4.5. References

BAILEY, ELIZABETH

1977 *Old Babylonian inheritance procedures reconsidered.* Unpublished MA thesis, University of Arizona, Tucson.

CHIERA, E.

1922 *Old Babylonian contracts.* Publications of the Babylonian Section, vol. 8/2. University Museum, University of Pennsylvania, Philadelphia.

DAVID, M.

1927 *Die Adoption im altbabylonischen Recht.* Leipziger rechtswissenschaftliche Studien, vol. 23. Verlag von Theodor Weicher, Leipzig.

DRIVER, G. R. and J. MILES

1952 *The Babylonian laws*, vol. 1, Legal commentary. Oxford University Press, Oxford.

EDZARD, D. O.

1957 *Die "zweite Zwischenzeit" Babyloniens.* Otto Harrassowitz, Wiesbaden.

FEIGIN, S.

1979 *Legal and administrative texts of the reign of Samsu-iluna.* Yale Oriental Series, Babylonian Texts, vol. 12. Yale University Press, New Haven.

FIGULLA, H. (and W. Martin)

1953 *Letters and documents of the Old-Babylonian period.* Ur Excavation Texts, vol. 5. Publications of the Joint Expedition of the British Museum and of the University Museum, University of Pennsylvania, Philadelphia, to Mesopotamia.

FINKELSTEIN, J. J.

1968 *Old Babylonian legal documents*. Cuneiform texts . . . in the British Museum, vol. 48. British Museum, London.

1976a *Šilip rēmim* and related matters. In *Cuneiform studies in honor of Samuel Noah Kramer*, edited by B. Eichler, pp. 187-194. Alter Orient und Altes Testament, vol. 25. Neukirchener Verlag, Neukirchen-Vluyn.

1976b Cutting the *sissiktu* in divorce proceedings. *Welt des Orients* 8:236-240.

FRANKENA, R.

1965 *Altbabylonische Briefe aus Lagaba*. Tabulae cuneiformes a F. M. Th. de Liagre Boehl collectae, vol. 4. E. J. Brill, Leiden.

GREENGUS, S.

1979 *Old Babylonian tablets from Ishchali and vicinity*. Nederlands Historisch-Archaeologisch Instituut te Istanbul.

HARRIS, R.

1977 Notes on the slave names of Old Babylonian Sippar. *Journal of Cuneiform Studies* 29:46-51.

KLENGEL, H.

1973 *Altbabylonische Rechts- und Wirtschaftsurkunden*. Vorderasiatische Schriftdenkmaeler der staatlichen Museen zu Berlin, vol. 18, Akademie-Verlag, Berlin.

KLÍMA, J. J.

1964 *Gesellschaft und Kultur des alten Mesopotamien*. Verlag der Tschechoslowakischen Akademie der Wissenschaften, Prague.

KOSCHAKER, P.

1931 *Ueber einige griechische Rechtsurkunden aus den oestlichen Randgebieten des Hellenismus, mit Beitraegen zum Eigentums- und Pfandbegriff nach griechischem und orientalischen Rechten*. Abhandlungen der Saechsischen Akademie der Wissenschaften, philologisch-historische Klasse, vol. 42/1. Verlag von S. Hirzel, Leipzig.

KRAUS, F. R.

1969a Von altmesopotamischem Erbrecht, ein Vortrag. In *Essays on oriental laws of succession*, pp. 1-17. Studia et documenta ad iura orientis antiqui pertinentia, vol. 9. E. J. Brill, Leiden.

1969b Erbrechtliche Terminologie im alten Mesopotamien, mit einem kritischen Beitrage von B. Landsberger. In *Essays on oriental laws of succession*, pp. 18-57. Studia et documenta ad iura orientis antiqui pertinentia, vol. 9. E. J. Brill, Leiden.

1973 *Vom mesopotamischen Menschen der altbabylonischen Zeit und seiner Welt*. North Holland Publishing Company, Amsterdam.

LANDSBERGER, B.

1937 *Die Serie ana ittišu*. Materalien zum sumerischen Lexikon, vol. 1. Pontifical Biblical Institute, Rome.

MEISSNER, B.

1893 *Beitraege zum altbabylonischen Privatrecht*. Assyriologische Bibliothek, vol. 11. Leipzig.

MENDELSOHN, I.

1949 *Slavery in the ancient Near East*. Oxford University Press, New York.

PINCHES, T.

1899 *Cuneiform texts from Babylonian tablets . . . in the British Museum*, vol. 8. British Museum, London.

POEBEL, A.

1909 *Babylonian legal and business documents from the time of the First Dynasty of Babylon, chiefly from Nippur*. The Babylonian Expedition of the University of Pennsylvania, Series A: Cuneiform Texts, vol. 6, part 2. University of Pennsylvania, Philadelphia.

VON PRAAG, A.

1945 *Droit matrimonial assyro-babylonien*. N. V. Noord-Hollandische Uitgevers Maatschappij, Amsterdam.

SCHORR, M.

1913 *Urkunden des altbabylonischen Zivil- und Prozessrechts*. Vorderasiatische Bibliothek, vol. 5. J. C. Hinrichs'sche Buchhandlung, Leipzig.

STAMM, J. J.

1939 *Die akkadische Namengebung*. Mitteilungen der Vorderasiatisch-Aegyptischen Gesellschaft, vol. 44. J. E. Hinrichs Verlag, Leipzig.

SZLECHTER, E.

1952 L'affranchissement en droit suméro-akkadien. *Revue internationale de droit de l'antiquité*, vol. 1:125-195.

UNGNAD, A.

1909 *Vorderasiatische schriftdenkmaeler der koeniglichen Museen zu Berlin*, vol. 9. J. C. Hinrichs'sche Buchhandlung, Leipzig.

WESTBROOK, R.

1975 *Old Babylonian family law*. Unpublished manuscript.

WILCKE, C. and R. KUTSCHER

1978 Eine Ziegel-Inschrift des Koenigs Takil-ilišsu von Malgium, gefunden in Isin und Yale. *Zeitschrift fuer assyriologie* 68:95-128.

CHAPTER 5

Ki 1056: LIVING TOGETHER IN OLD BABYLONIAN KISH

Ki 1056, B 466 in the *PRAK* I catalogue, was briefly summarized by de Genouillac as a "beau fragment d'une très grande tablette (epaisseur, 55 mm), liste pour paiement de gens par 'maison'." De Genouillac did not in fact copy this text although, even in fragmentary condition, it is one of the most visually impressive specimens in the Kish collection and certainly the largest. Perhaps the lack of a copy can be attributed to the cursive and very small script and the absence of any literary character or grammatical peculiarity to the text. This text, nevertheless, is a unique document, providing substantial information on Old Babylonian family structure of a sort not otherwise encountered in this period (cf. Gelb et al., forthcoming). We present here a hand-copy of the text (figs. 23-24) and photographs (pl. VI) to accompany the following edition and comments.

5.1. Transliteration

Obverse, 4 columns

	Col. I			Household
1′	[	]	dumu-géme	
2′		[é	x]-^{d}nin-gal	A.
3′	[x]	x]-*ma-za-tum*	dam-ni	
4′	[	*x*-]-*hu-ya*	géme-ni	
5′	[	x]-*bi-it*	dumu-ni	
6′	[	x]-*ni*	dumu-ni	
7′	[	x]	dumu-ni	
8′		[é	]-*bu*(?)	B.
		rest of column lost		

	Col. II			Household
1′	[	⸢x-x⸣		
2′	[ ]	*ṣa-pu-ur-tum*	dam!-ni	
3′	⸢3 bán⸣	*bi-it-ta-tum*	dumu-munus-ni	
4′	2 bán	*ab-di-a-ra-ah*	šeš-ni	

Col. II				Household
5′		é ^{d}EN.ZU-*ma-gir*		C.
6′	1 PI 3 bán	*pù-zur*$_8$-^{d}EŠ$_4$.DAR		
7′		dumu *da-zu-zum*		
8′	3 bán	*ya-di-da-tum*	dam-ni	
9′	3 bán	*a-ha-sú-nu*	é-gi-a	
10′		é *pù-zur*$_8$-^{d}EŠ$_4$.DAR		D.
11′	2 PI	*a-hu-ši-na*		
		dumu *du-qú-qum*		
12′	[ ]	*ma-na-tum*	dam-ni	
13′	[	*šu*]*m-ma-an-la*-^{d}UTU	dumu-ni	
14′	[ ]	⌜*a*⌝-*hu-na-tum*	géme-ni	
15′	[	x]-*mi-is*-AN	dumu-ni	
16′		[é *a-hu-ši-na*]		E.
		rest of column lost		

Col. III				Household
1′		é *a-ki-ya*		F.
2′	3 bán	^{d}*eš-har-ga-me-la-at*		
			dam-ni	
3′	2 bán	*a-ha-sú-nu*	dumu-munus-ni	
4′	2 bán	*i-ku-pí*-^{d}IM	dumu-ni	
5′	1 bán 5 sìla	^{d}UTU-*an-dùl-li*	dumu-ni	
6′		é *iš-me*-^{d}IM		G.
7′	3 bán	*hu-mu-si*	dam-ni	
8′	2 bán	*i-bi*-^{d}IM	dumu-ni	
9′	2 bán	*tab-ni*-ES$_4$.DAR	dumu-munus-ni	
10′	1 bán 5 sìla	*ra-bi-ṣíl-la-šu*	dumu-ni	
11′	2 bán	*mu-na-wi-ir-tum*	géme-ni	
12′	1 bán	*ad-ma-at-ì-lí*	dumu-ni	
13′		é ^{d}EN.ZU-*iš-me-ni*		H.

Col. III				Household
14′	1 PI 3 bán	ARAD$_2$-*ì-lí-ya*		
		dumu *la-li-ya*		
15′	3 bán	*a-mur-ri-tum*	d[am-ni]	
16′	2 bán	*a-di*-AN$^{(?)}$-[	dumu-ni]	
17′	[x	x x	]	I.
		rest of column lost		

Col. IV				Household
1′	[x	x x x˺-*ì-lí*	dumu-ni	
2′	1 bán	*za-ni-nu-um*	dumu-ni	
3′		é ^{d}EN.ZU-*na-ši*		J.
4′	1 PI 3 bán	*da-da-nu-um*		
		dumu *la-li-ya*		
5′	3 bán	*ar-wi-a*	dam-ni	
6′	2 bán	*a-ha-ti-wa-qar-at*	géme-ni	
7′	2 bán	*ap-pá-an*-AN	dumu-ni	
8′	2 bán	*hu-mu-si*	nin-ni	
9′		é *da-da-nu-um*		K.
10′	1 PI 4 bán	[householder	]	
11′	3 bán	[	(?) dam-ni]	
12′	3 bán	[	(?)]	
13′	2 bán	[	(?) dumu-(munus)-ni]	
14′	2 bán	[	(?) dumu-(munus)-ni]	L.
15′	[ ]	rest of column lost		

Reverse, 4 columns

Col. V				Household
1′	3 bán	[	(?) dam-ni]	
2′	2 bán	[	(?) dumu-(munus)-ni]	
3′	1 bán 5 sila	a[-x	(?) dumu-gaba]	

	Col. V			Household
4′		é *a-hi-ki-ba-ni*		M.
5′	3 bán	*ša-at-*^{d}MAR.TU		
6′	3 bán	*a-li-ah-hu-ša*	dumu-munus-ni	
7′	2 bán	*hu-mu-si*	dumu-munus-ni	
8′	1 bán 5 sìla	*hu-na-ba-tum*	dumu-munus-ni	
9′	1 bán 5 sìla	*bur-ru-kam*	dumu-gaba	
10′		é *ša-at-*<^{d}> MAR.TU		N.
11′	3 bán	*ya-ya-tum*	ama-ni	
12′	3 bán	*nu-na-tum*	é-gi-a	
13′	[ ]	⸢x x x x⸣	géme-ni	O.
		rest of column lost		

	Col. VI			Household
1′	[x bán		]	
2′	2 bán	[x	]	
3′	2 bán	^{d}*eš-ha*[*r-ga-me-la-*]		
		-at	[? dumu-munus-ni]	
4′		é ^{d}ÍD-*bi-tum*		P.
5′	1 PI 2 bán	*nu-úr-*EŠ$_4$.DAR		
		dumu *gu-gu-um*		
6′	3 bán	*da-aq-qar-tum*	dam-ni	
7′	2 bán	*nu-ra-tum*	dumu-munus-ni	
8′	1 bán 5 sìla	*ka-am-ma-ni*	dumu-munus-ni	
9′		é *nu-úr-*EŠ$_4$.DAR		Q.
10′	1 PI 2 bán	*mi-in-ni-nu-um*		
		dumu *ha-an-nu-ú-um*		
11′	3 bán	*na-ku-ur-tum*	dam-ni	
12′	2 bán	*a-hu-um-wa-qar*	dumu-ni	
13′	2 bán	ARAD$_2$-^{d}EN.ZU	[dumu-ni]	
14′		[é *mi-in-ni-nu-um*]		R.
		rest of column lost		

Col. VII				Household
1′	[	*ku-ru-um-tum*]		
		[dumu] x-*i-lí-a*		
2′	[	-x] *-tum*	nin-dingir ^{d}IM	
3′	[	-x] *-dùl-la-ni*	šeš	
4′		é *ku-ru-um-tum*		S.
5′	3 bán	É.A-*la-ma-sí*	dam$^{!}$-ni	
6′	3 bán	EŠ$_4$.DAR- *ra-bi-a-at*	dumu-munus-ni	
7′	3 bán	*ta-ku-ur-tum*	dumu-munus-ni	
8′	2 bán	AN-*ti*-PI-*tum-um-mi*	nin-ni	
9′	1 bán 5.sìla	*na-ru-ub-tum*	nin-<ni>	
10′	1 bán	*a-bu-wa-qar*	dumu-gaba	
11′		é *ìl-šu-ba-ni*		T.
12′		GI$_6$-*lí*-^{d}EN.ZU		
		dumu *la-li-ya*		
13′	[	*x x*] *-tum*	dam-ni	
	[		d] umu-munus-ni	U.
		rest of column lost		

Col. VIII				Household
1′	[	]	dumu-ni	V.
2′	[		dumu-] munus-ni	
		rest lost		

5.2. Structure of the Text

As only the fragment of a much larger document, Ki 1056 preserves twenty-two separate sections, eleven of which are completely intact. Each section represents the household (é = *bītum*) of a person. The largest households (e.g., E, H, K) are composed of a man (named with his patronym), his wife, his children, his female slave, and her children, and other adults in the household. An amount of produce, presumably barley, is listed before each individual and the individuals are ranked in strict descending order according to the amount of produce they receive. Following the last entry of family members a line is drawn, a small space is left and then the phrase é (*bīt*) PN (the name of the family head) is written. Four households may be used as examples of this structure.

E.

120 liters	Ahušina, son of Duququm
[liters]	Manatum, his wife
[liters]	Šummanlašamaš, his son
[liters]	Ahunatum, his female slave
[liters]	X-mis-ilum(?), her son

[Household of Ahušina]

K.

90 liters	Dadanum, son of Laliya
30 liters	Arwi'a, his wife
20 liters	Ahatiwaqrat, his female slave
20 liters	Appanili, her son
20 liters	Humusi, his sister (?)

Household of Dadanum

In some cases the first entry in the household is not the householder, but his wife:

H.

30 liters	Humusi, his wife
20 liters	Ibbi'adad, his son
20 liters	Tabni'ištar, his daughter
15 liters	Rabiṣillašu, his son
20 liters	Munawirtum, female slave
10 liters	Admatili, her son

Household of Sinišmeni

It may be inferred that the male head of the household, Sinišmeni, is absent, perhaps on military or corvée duties, at the time this text was written. This interpretation seems justified since Humusi receives the standard portion for wives and is not described as the head of the household; although there is no adult male in the household, Munawirtum, his slave, and her son are recorded. In household N, on the other hand, in which no male is listed, the absence is for a different reason.

N.

30 liters	Šatamurrim
30 liters	Ali'ahhuša, her daughter
20 liters	Humusi, her daughter
15 liters	Hunabatum, her daughter
15 liters	Burrukam, infant

Household of Šatamurrim

In this section we may think that Šatamurrim is a widow, since she not only leads the section as the first recipient of grain, but also is explicitly denoted as the head of the household.

The amount of grain male heads of households receive, 80-120 liters, is more than twice to four times the amount received by anyone else in the text. Gelb (et al., forthcoming) suggests that these amounts correspond roughly to the monthly ration rates listed in Ur III texts; it may be provisionally considered, then, that Ki 1056 was a monthly account.

5.3. Family Structure

The families recorded in this text are monogamous, only one husband and one wife comprise each household. In household S, it would seem that Kurrumtum (the name is gramatically feminine) is unmarried, and, as noted above, widows could be householders. Slave women are listed in five texts and in each case (save O which is incomplete) have born children. It is certain that the children listed after the slave's entry are her children since in household A, though broken, the name immediately preceding that of the head of household is clearly glossed dumu géme(=*mār amtim*). No adult male slaves are members of these households, although all the names of the children of the slave women are in fact male.

The "other adults" who appear as family members are infrequent in number. AMA (=*ummum*), "mother" is included in household O. In this incompletely preserved section, Yayatum is the first entry and there seems to be no wife, but a *kallatum* (see below) and a slave are recorded. The sign AMA is in fact very cursive, but Donbaz's copy can be easily verified with reference to the photograph. In household T a similar sign appears, but we have interpreted it to be an elision with the -zi preceding it; we have consequently read the sign dam which fits the context of this section.

Also in household T are two "sisters," nin(=*ahatum*). In the cursive script of this document the signs NIN and DAM seem indistinguishable. If Ealamassi is the wife of Ilšubani, however, the two women (one of whose name is obscure) listed after the two daughters of the householder may be interpreted as his sisters. Another sister appears in household K. "Brothers," šeš(=*ahum*), are recorded in households C and S, in both cases following all other listings in the section.

In households D and O the kinship term é-gi-a(=*kallatum*; usually written é-gi_4-a, but see *CAD* under *kallatum*) is found. The word is usually translated "bride (-to be)" or "daughter-in-law." In both sections O and D, no males are present and thus "daughter-in-law" seems impossible. It seems likelier, with no information to the contrary, to regard *kallatum* here as denoting "bride," a girl betrothed to a man but still living in her father's house. She is given 30 liters rations, more than a child, and is not classified as a "daughter."

The last two terms to be discussed are dumu-gaba (=*mār irtim/dumugabu*), "infant," in households M, N and T and nin-dingir (*ugbabtu*) Adad in S. dumu-gaba is restored in M on the basis of the 15 liters of grain recorded for a broken entry in that section. The infant listed in N receives 15 liters and the one in T 10 liters. In N and T the infant is the last of the entries and receives the smallest portion of grain. No slaves appear in these texts. The *ugbabtu*-devotee of Adad (a divinity who appears in many of the personal names throughout this text) is presumably an unmarried sister of Kurumtum, female head of household S whose (unmarried) brother is also recorded. It is moot whether the *ugbabtum* of Adad lived in the house or was rather allocated grain on the basis of her family membership (cf. Renger 1967:144-149; Klengel 1971:124-129).

Finally under the topic of family structure, it must be pointed out that several of the families denoted in this text were related. Three householders, Waradiliya (I), Dadanum (K), and Ṣillisin (U) were sons of Laliya.

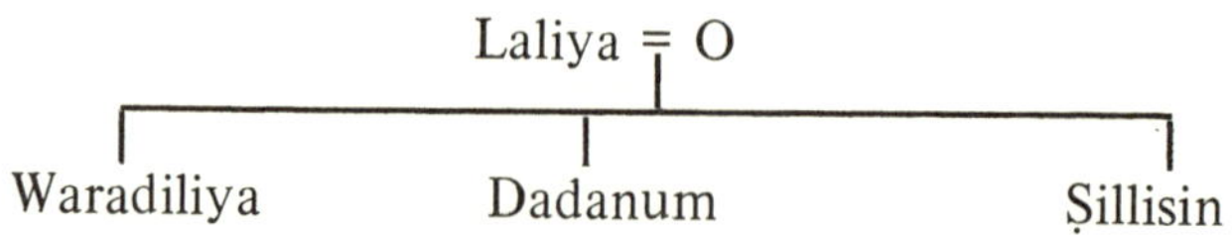

The possible reason three agnatically related nuclear families were grouped in this document will be explored in our discussion which follows tables of the names found in Ki 1056.

Table 7. Index of Personal Names

Abdiʾarah	C	Humusi	K	Šatamurrim	N
Abuwaqar	T	Humusi	N	Ṣillisin	U
Admatili	H	Hunabatum	N	Sinišmeni	H
Ahassunu	D			Sinmagir	C
Ahassunu	G	Ibbiʾadad	H	Sinnaši	J
Ahatiwaqrat	K	ÍD-bitum	P	Šummanlašamaš	E
Ahikibani	M	Ikuppiʿadad	G		
Ahumwaqar	R	Ilšubani	T	Tabniʾištar	H
Ahunatum	E	Išmeʾadad	G	Takurtum	T
Ahušina	E	Ištarrabiʾat	T		
Akiya	F			Waradiliya	I
Aliʾahhuša	N	Kammani	Q	Waradsin	R
Amurritum	I	Kurumtum	S		
AN-ti-PI-tum-ummi	T			Yadidatum	D
Appanili	K	Laliya	I, K, U	Yayatum	O
Arwiʾa	K				
		Manatum	E	Zaninum	J
Bittatum	C	Minninum	R		
Burrukam	N	Munawirtum	H	a-x	M
				a-di-AN-x	I
Dadanum	K	Nakurtum	R	x-bi-it	B
Daqqartum	Q	Narubtum	T	-bu(?)	B
Dazuzum	D	Nunatum	O	x-dùl-la-ni	S
Duququm	E	Nuratum	Q	x-ì-lí	J
		Nurištar	Q	x-ì-lí-ya	S
Ealamassi	T			-hu-ya	B
Ešhargamelat	G	Puzurištar	D	-ma-za-tum	B
Ešhargamelat	P			x-mi-is-AN	E
		Rabiṣillašu	H	x-ni	B
Gugum	Q			x-^{d}nin-gal	A
		Šamašandulli	G	-tum	S
Ḫannum	R	Ṣapurtum	C	-tum	U

Table 8. Kinship Identifications

Name	Household
Householders	
-^{d}nin-gal	A
-bu(?)	B
Sinmagir	C
Puzurištar	D
Ahušina	E
Akiya	F
Išme᾿adad	G
Sinišmeni	H
Waradiliya	I
Sinnaši	J
Dadanum	K
Ahikibani	M
Šatamurrim	N
ÍD-bi-tum	P
Nurištar	Q
Minninum	R
Kurumtum	S
Ilšubani	T
Ṣillisin	U
Wives	
-ma-za-tum	B
Ṣapurtum	C
Yadidatum	D
Manatum	E
Ešhargamelat	G
Humusi	H
Amurritum	I
Arwi᾿a	K
Daqqartum	Q
Nakurtum	R
Ealamassi	T
-tum	U
Male children	
Šummanlašamaš	E
Ikuppi᾿adad	G
Šamašandulli	G
Ibbi᾿adad	H
Rabiṣillašu	H
x-ili	J
Zaninum	J
Ahumwaqar	R
Waradsin	R
x	V
Female children	
Bittatum	C
Ahassunu	G
Tabni᾿ištar	H
Ali᾿ahhuša	N
Humusi	N
Hunabatum	N
Ešhargamelat(?)	P
Nuratum	Q
Kammani	Q
Ištarrabi᾿at	T
Takurtum	T
x	U
x	V
Children of uncertain gender	
two or three(?)	L
A-di-AN(?)-x	I
one	M
Infants	
a-x(?)	M
Burrukam	N
Abuwaqar	T
Slaves	
x-hu-ya	B
Aḫuratum	E
Munawirtum	H
Ahatiwaqrat	K
x	O
Children of slaves	
x	A
x-bi-it	B
x-ni	B
x	B
x-mi-is-AN	E
Admatili	H
Appanili	K
Other adults	
šeš(=*ahum*)	
Abdi᾿arah	C
x-dùl-la-ni	S
nin(=*ahatum*)	
Humusi	K
AN-ti-PI-tum-um-mi	T
Narubtum	T
ama(=*ummum*)	
Yayatum	O
é-gi-a(=*kallatum*)	
Ahassunu	D
Nunatum	O
nin-dingir ^{d}IM(=*ugbabti Adad*)	
x-tum	S

5.4. On Living Together in Kish

Over about the last fifteen years, it has become something of a commonplace in Assyriological literature that extended family units in early Mesopotamia played important roles in the economic and social landscapes during the third millennium B.C. (e.g., Oppenheim 1964:77; Gelb 1967, 1969; Diakonoff 1971, 1975, 1976). For example, in a recent study Steinkeller has argued that the Fara-Sargonic period land-sale documents exemplify the institution of the common ownership of land, and that the three payments found in typical texts represent the price proper, the additional payments to the seller's (consanguineal?) relatives, and gifts intended to integrate the buyer with the seller and his whole kinship group (Steinkeller 1977).

In the second millennium B.C., however, many analysts seem to take for granted that whatever extended family relationships may have existed in an earlier time have now attenuated (Gelb 1967:6; Oppenheim 1964:77-79). This opinion appears to rest partly on the well-disseminated studies of urban sociologists of the 1930s and 40s who considered that ascribed kin-ties tend to be of little importance in cities (e.g., Wirth 1938:20-21). These studies, however, have been largely controverted by more recent and varied analyses of large cities in developing nations, particularly in sub-Saharan Africa (e.g., Lloyd, Magobunje, and Awe:1967). Theoretically, the question of kinship relations in urban environments is now open, and it is in this light that the Mesopotamian case(s) must be evaluated.

In addition to Ki 1056, other texts which treat various groups of people as corporate entities and words that refer to social associations are, in fact, not uncommon in the Old Babylonian period. One of the most important examples of such a text is the one published by Gelb and entitled by him, "An Old Babylonian list of Amorites" (Gelb 1968). From Ešnunna and dating to the early part of the Old Babylonian period, it enumerates twenty-nine individuals of the Amoritical persuasion, divided into five *babtum*'s and denoted as residing in the city. Gelb translated *babtum*, each of which bears the name of an individual, as "small encampment" or "section," against the *CAD*'s "quarter of a city". According to Gelb, the *babtum* "probably [was] restricted to the individuals belong to a certain tribal grouping" (Gelb 1968:43).

The concept of *babtum*, as indicated by Gelb, does not necessarily describe a geographical situation in a city, proximity to a city-gate or a city-quarter, and does not connote a territory bounded for purposes of political struggle as translations of "city-ward" anachronistically seem to convey. Rather, as Oppenheim has noted, a *babtum* consisted of a "community of families . . . a corporation which could sell real estate, decide legal cases, write letters to kings, and receive messages from them" (Oppenheim 1969:8). Thus, in the "code" of Hammurabi, *babtum* is cited in several paragraphs, almost always in the context of some corporate responsibility for a member's malfeasance, or noncompliance with certain existing demand-rights and privileges in the area of family and other social relations. At present the defining quality of membership in a *babtum* can only be conjectured, but the very appearance of this sort of social institution in Mesopotamian cities is in itself worth discussing.

In comparing Gelb's "list of Amorites" with a text mentioning a *rabiʾan babtīšu*, M. Stol has assumed that these 'small encampments' (Gelb) were headed by a *rabiʾānum*, now 'alderman' (Stol 1976:80; note, however, that *rabiʾānum* does not appear in Gelb's text). Stol's two translations of *rabiʾānum*, "sheikh" and "alderman" (he also translates "burgomaster"), clearly derive from the model of the progressive sedentism of nomads: the headman is "sheikh" in the more mobile stage, and "alderman/burgomaster" when the social group is fully settled.

In our view this explanation of the *babtum* and the model of the progressive sedentism of nomads in the Old Babylonian period lacks convincing force. Without becoming embroiled here in the lengthy and important debate on the "Amorite question" (cf. Kamp and Yoffee 1980), nor being able to resume the no less significant arguments concerning nomadic-sedentary relations in Mesopotamian history, we only want to make a few minor points and to present a cautionary tale. In the Ešnunna text discussed by Gelb, in which Amorites are explicitly designated as such, and clearly denoted as living in a city, it is certainly a reasonable conclusion that being an Amorite was a particular distinguishing feature, that not all Amorites lived in cities, and that Amorites were often grouped by *babtum*. In the "code" of Hammurabi, however, one does not gain the impression that *babtum*s were restricted to Amorites, but in fact one might infer that *babtum*s were integral units in Mesopotamian cities (cf. Kraus 1973:59).

As an alternative hypothesis to the notion that corporate, familial groups in Mesopotamian cities are only vestiges of a nomadic past, we might consider that the existence of *babtum*s and other such groups in Mesopotamian cities (cf. Kraus 1973:46-49; Oppenheim 1969) implies a certain normative network of kinship bonds in those settings. Now by kinship we mean not only exclusive biological descent relationships, but also the formulation of political and social alliances among groups and the allocation of special roles and property. Lineages and genealogies are in any event far more political histories than they are biological lines. For example, the significance of the dynastic lists of Hammurabi and Šamši-Adad (cf. Finkelstein 1966) is not that they are disinterested remembrances of distant ancestors, but that they reflect carefully conceived tracts of political propaganda designed partly to unify independent groups into a functioning sociopolitical system (cf. Kamp and Yoffee 1980).

In the time of the reign of Hammurabi (or shortly before) in Kish, when we suppose Ki 1056 was written, we have presented evidence that groups of related people lived together in Mesopotamian cities and that provisions were allocated to them according to social units. Households were considered reserved for nuclear families, but several related families were bound together into larger associations. These associations were *perhaps* called *babtum*s, and, as can be seen from the "code" of Hammurabi, had their own jurisdictions and responsibilities. Insofar as it may help to focus on the many problems involved in how Mesopotamians lived together in the second millennium B.C., therefore Ki 1056 finds its importance. The form and function of Mesopotamian habitational and relational patterns are among the areas most difficult of access to Assyriologists and Near Eastern archaeologists, and consequently are among the most neglected subjects in these fields. Nevertheless, these areas contain some of the most fundamental questions that need to be posed if we are ever to penetrate beyond the lives and deeds of royal personages and into the character of Mesopotamian history and social organization.

5.5. References

DIAKONOFF, I. M.

1976 "Slaves, helots and serfs in early antiquity." In *Wirtschaft und Gesellschaft im alten Vorderasien*, J. Harmatta and G. Komoróczy, eds., 45-78. Akadémiai Kiadó, Budapest.

1975 "The rural community in the ancient Near East." *Journal of the Economic and Social History of the Orient* 18:121-133.

1971 "On the structure of Old Babylonian society." In *Beiträge zur sozialen Struktur des alten Vorderasien*, H. Klengel, ed., 15-31. Akademie Verlag, Berlin.

FINKELSTEIN, J. J.

1966 "The genealogy of the Hammurabi dynasty." *Journal of Cuneiform Studies* 29:95-118.

GELB, I. J.

1969 "On the alleged temple and state economies in ancient Mesopotamia." In *Studi in Onore di Edoardo Volterra*, vol. 6, 137-154.

1968 "An Old Babylonian list of Amorites." *Journal of the American Oriental Society* 88:39-46.

1967 "Approaches to the study of ancient society." *Journal of the American Oriental Society* 87:1-8.

forthcoming *Sourcebook for the social and economic history of the ancient Near East.*

KAMP, K. A. and N. YOFFEE

1980 "Ethnicity in ancient Western Asia during the early second millennium B.C.: archaeological assessments of ethnoarchaeological prospectives." *Bulletin of the American Schools of Oriental Research* no. 238:85-104.

KLENGEL, H.

1971 "Drei altbabylonische Urkunden betreffend Felder von *ugbabtum*–Priesterinnen." *Journal of Cuneiform Studies* 23:124-129.

KRAUS, F. R.

1973 *Vom mesopotamischen Menschen der altbabylonischen Zeit und seiner Welt.* Mededelingen der Koninklijke Nederlandse Akademie van Wetenschappen, Afd. Letterkunde. Nieuwe Reeks-Deel 36–No. 6. North-Holland Publishing Company, Amsterdam.

LLOYD, P. C. and A. L. MABOGUNJE and B. AWE

1967 *The City of Ibadan.* University of Cambridge Press, Cambridge.

OPPENHEIM, A. L.

1964 *Ancient Mesopotamia. Portrait of a Dead Civilization.* University of Chicago Press, Chicago.

1969 "Mesopotamia–Land of Many Cities." In *Middle Eastern Cities*, I. M. Lapidus, ed., 3-18. University of California Press, Berkeley-Los Angeles.

RENGER, J.

1967 "Untersuchungen zum Priestertum in der altbabylonischen Zeit, I. Teil." *Zeitschrift für Assyriologie* 58:110-118.

STEINKELLER, P.

1977 "Some notes on the sale of real property in ancient Mesopotamia." Paper read at the 187th meeting of the American Oriental Society, Ithaca, N.Y. April 1977.

STOL, M.

1976 *Studies in Old Babylonian History.* Vitgaven van het Nederlands historisch-archaeologisch instituut te Istanbul XL. Leiden.

WIRTH, L.

1938 "Urbanism as a way of life." *American Journal of Sociology* 44:1-24.

Ki. 46

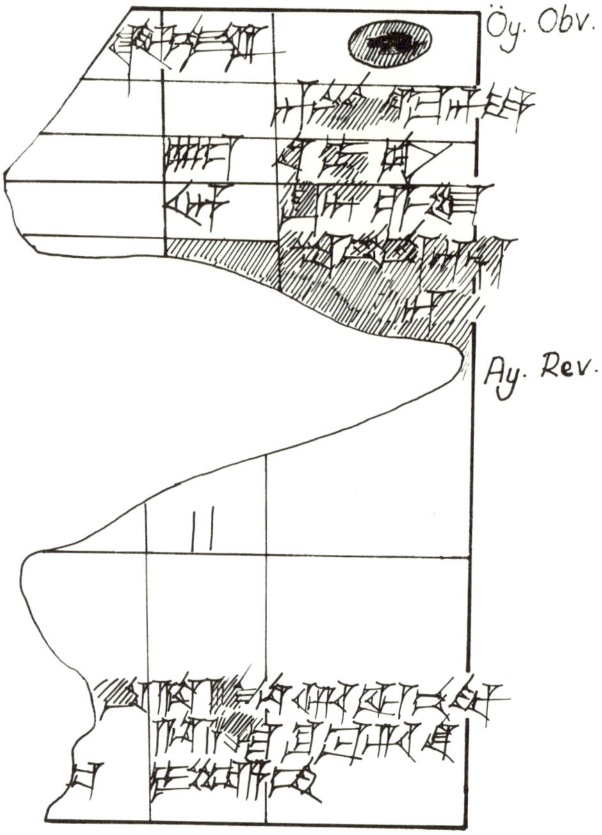

Ki. 73

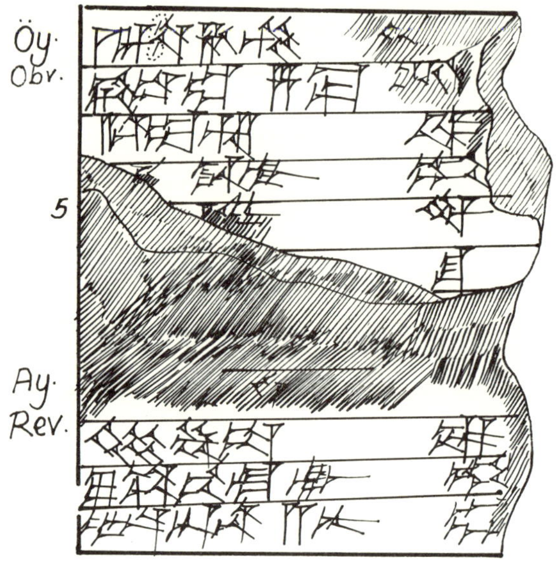

Ki. 591

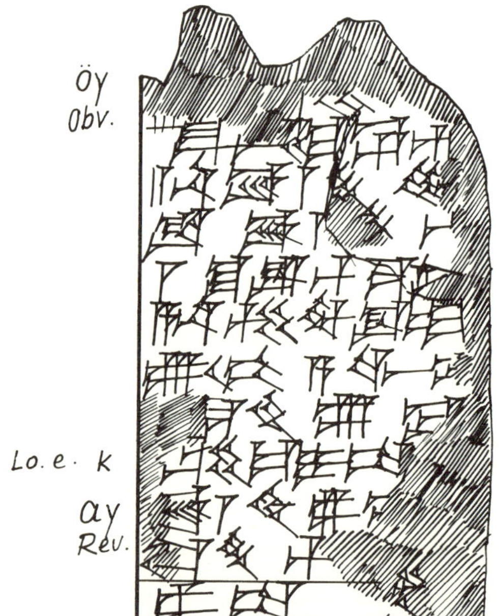

Ki. 78

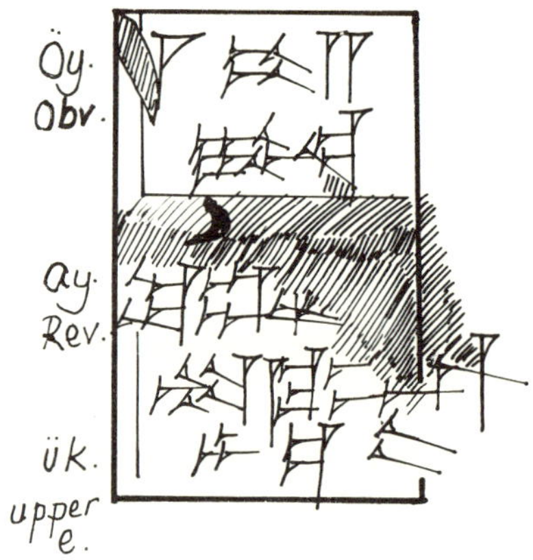

sol kenardaki mühür
seal on the left edge

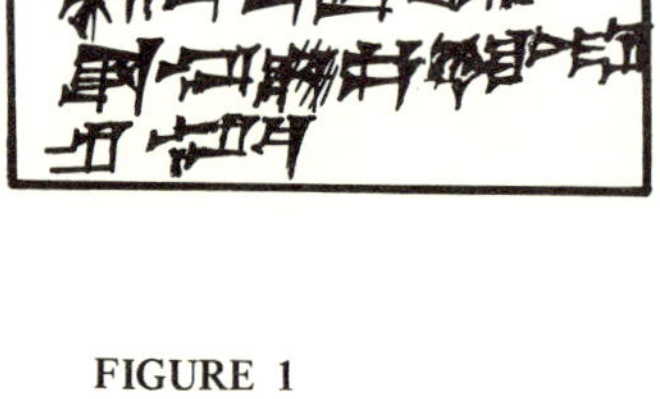

FIGURE 1

FIGURE 2

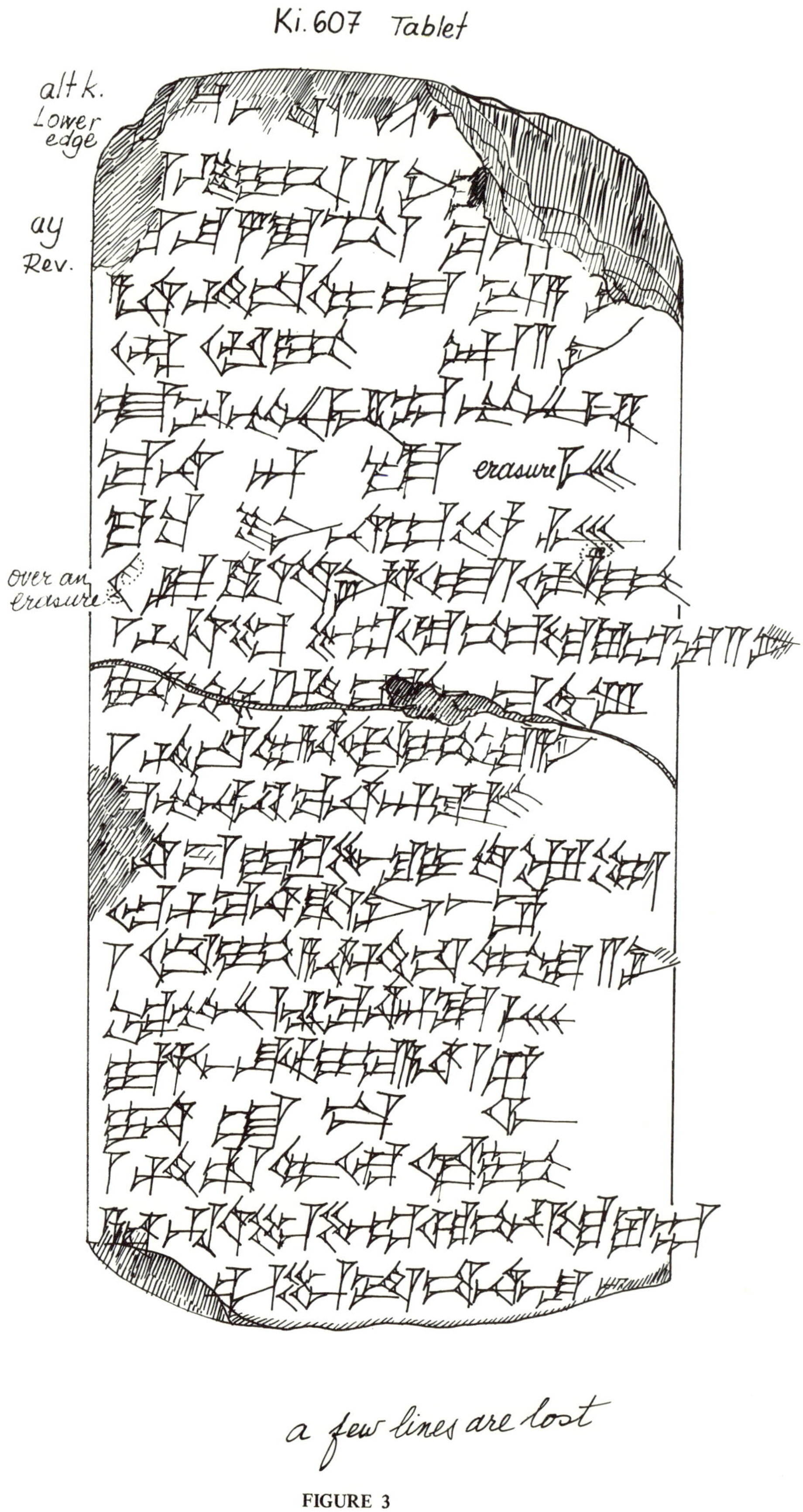
Ki. 607 Tablet
alt k.
Lower edge
ay
Rev.
erasure
over an erasure
a few lines are lost

FIGURE 3

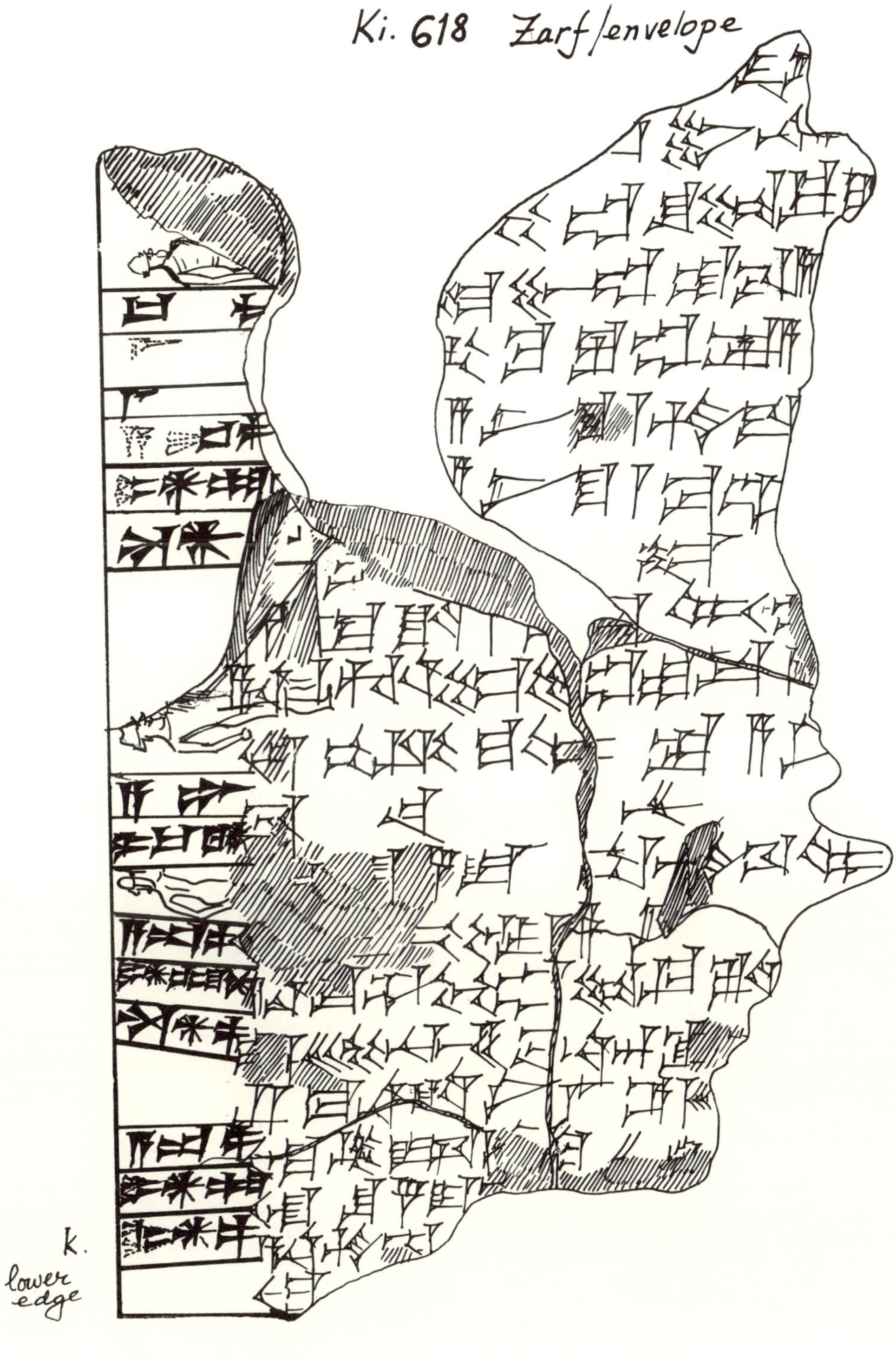

FIGURE 4

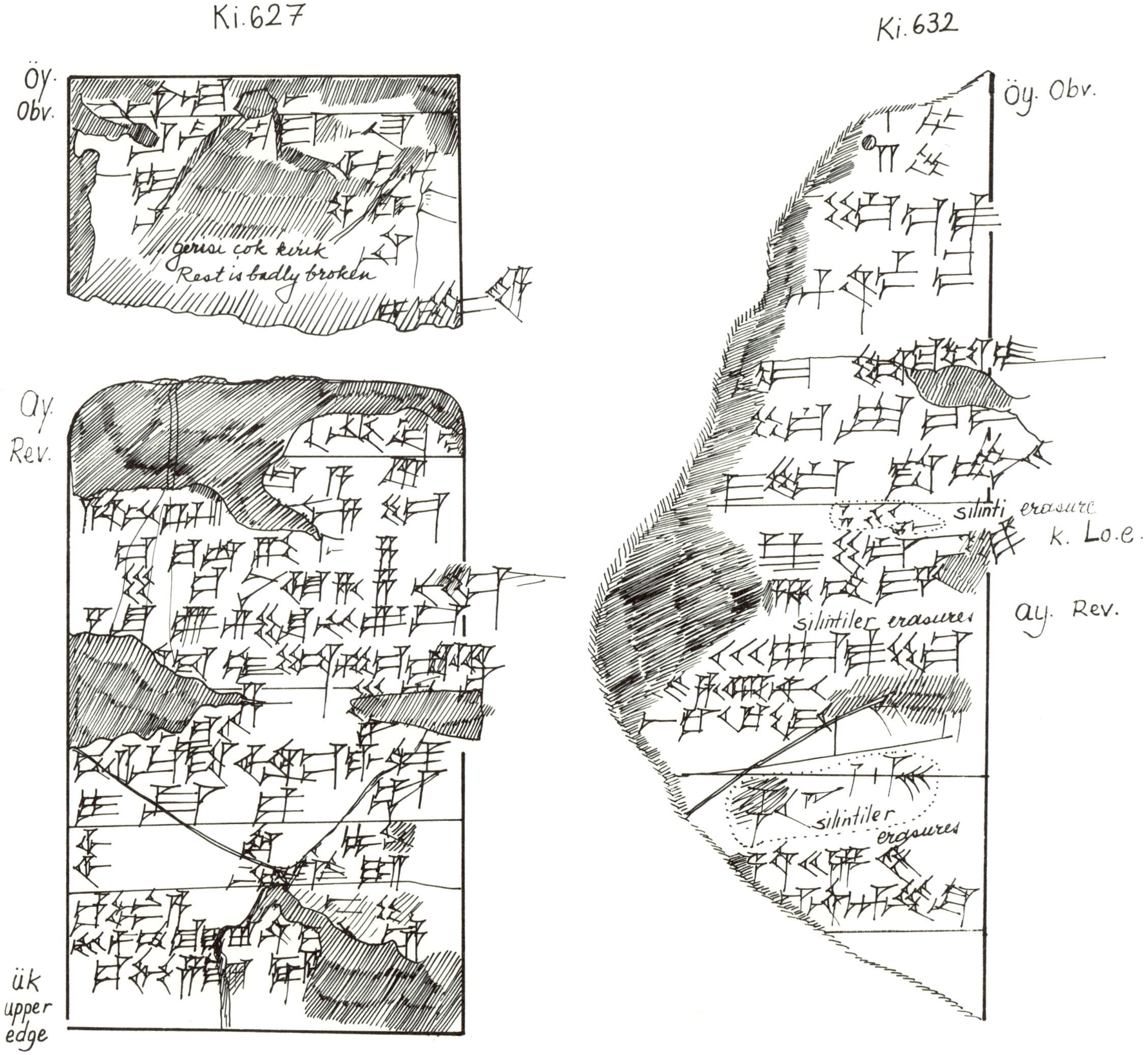
Ki.627
Öy. Obv.
gerisi çok kırık
Rest is badly broken
Ay. Rev.
ük upper edge
Ki.632
Öy. Obv.
silinti erasure
k. Lo.e.
ay. Rev.
silintiler erasures
silintiler erasures

FIGURE 5

Ki.645

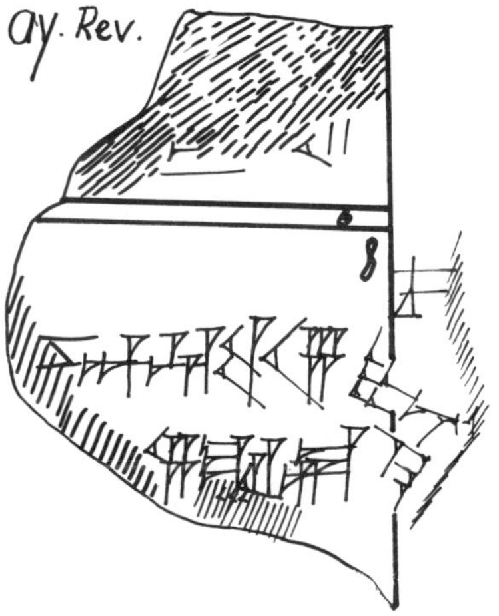

Ki.656

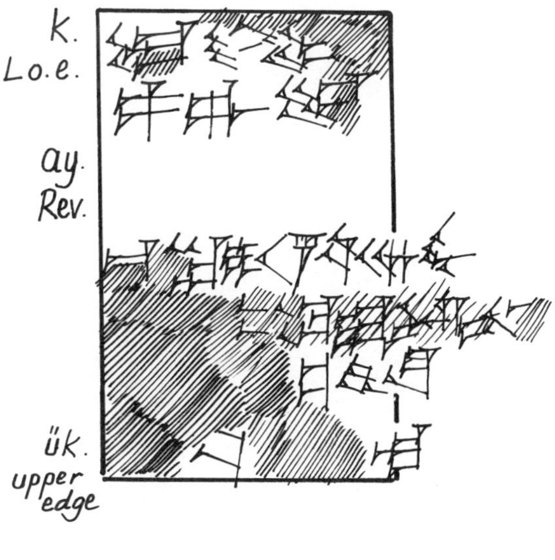

Ki.660

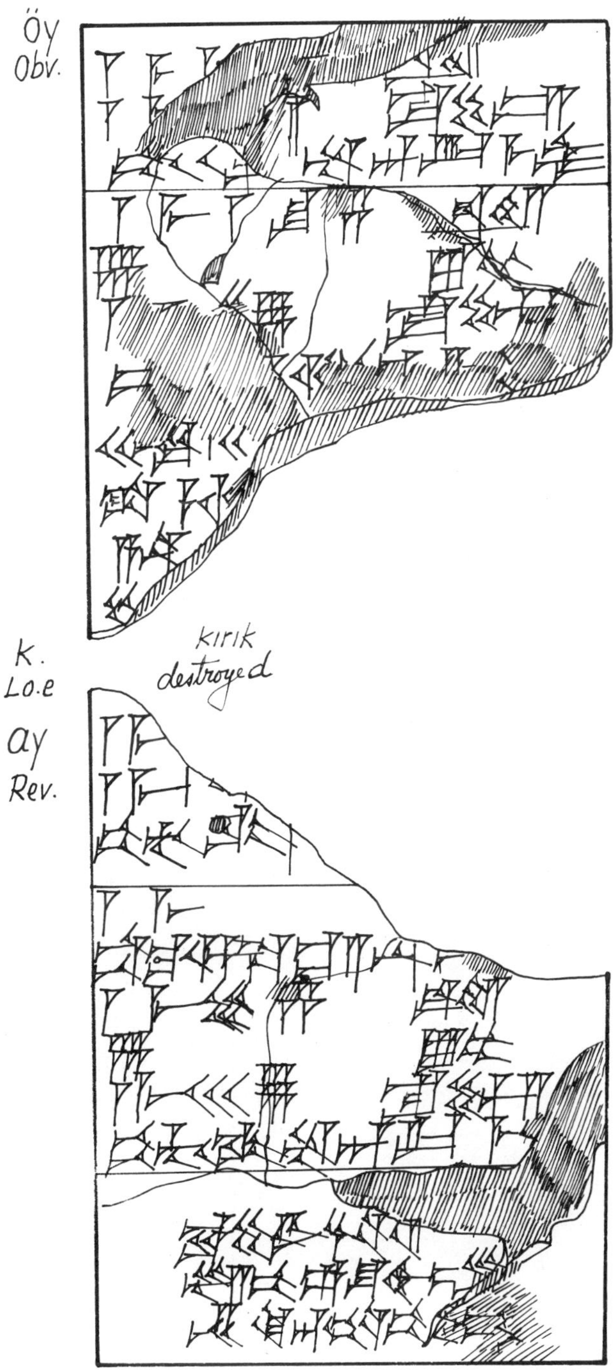

FIGURE 6

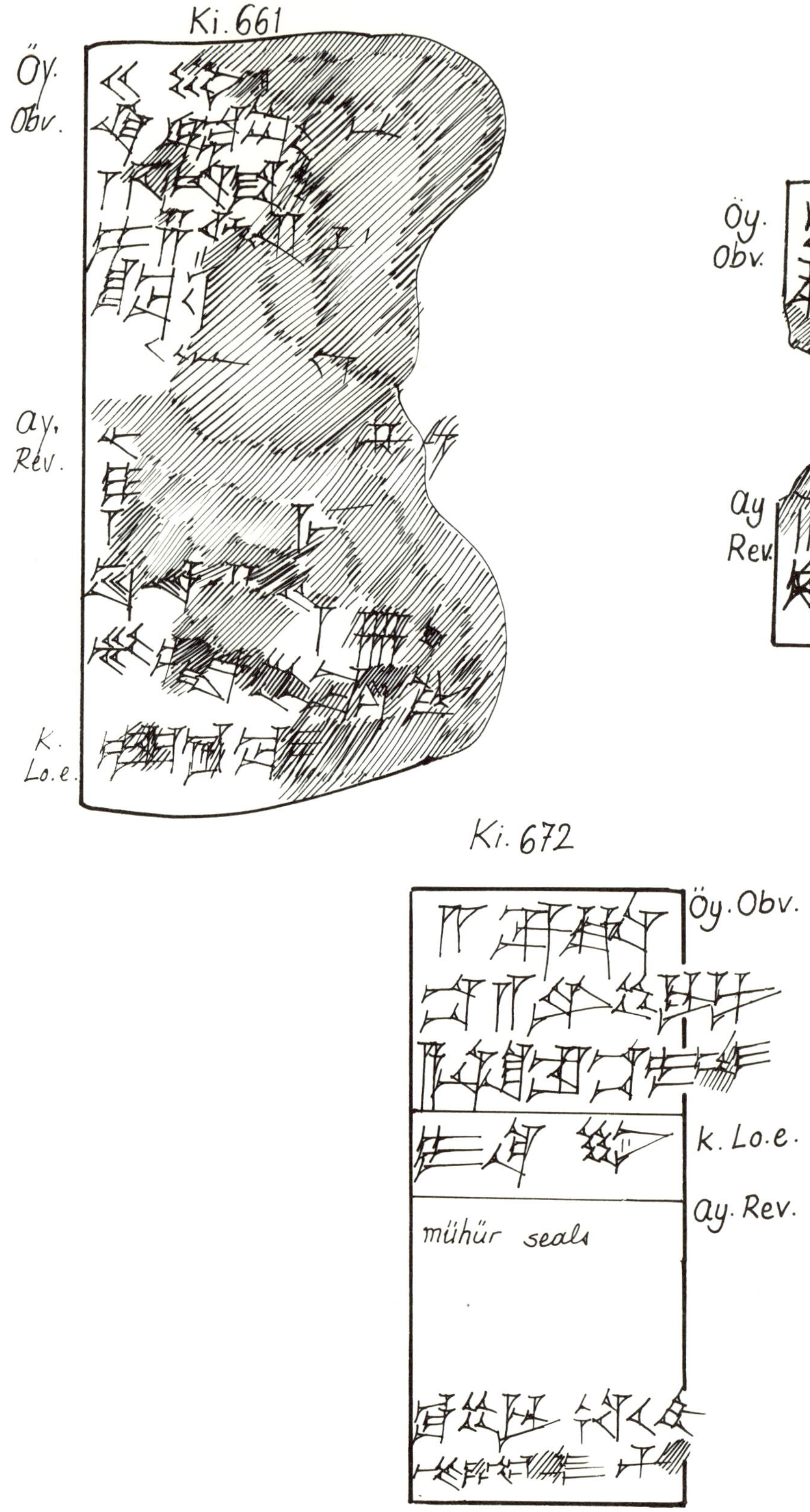
Ki. 661
Öy. Obv.
ay. Rev.
k. Lo.e.
Ki. 667
Öy. Obv.
ay Rev.
Ki. 672
Öy. Obv.
k. Lo.e.
ay. Rev.
mühür seals

FIGURE 7

Ki. 729

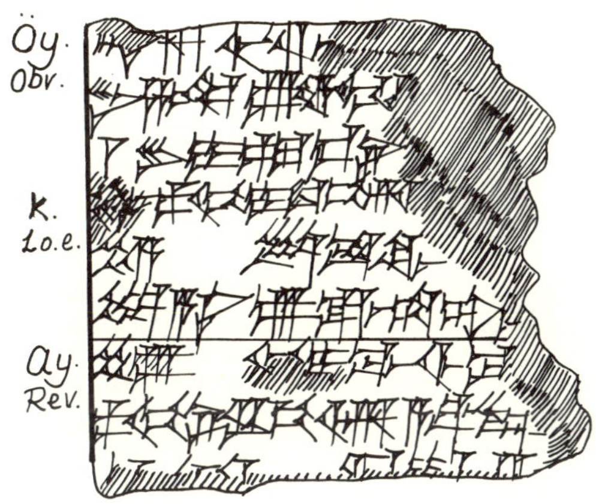

Ki. 730

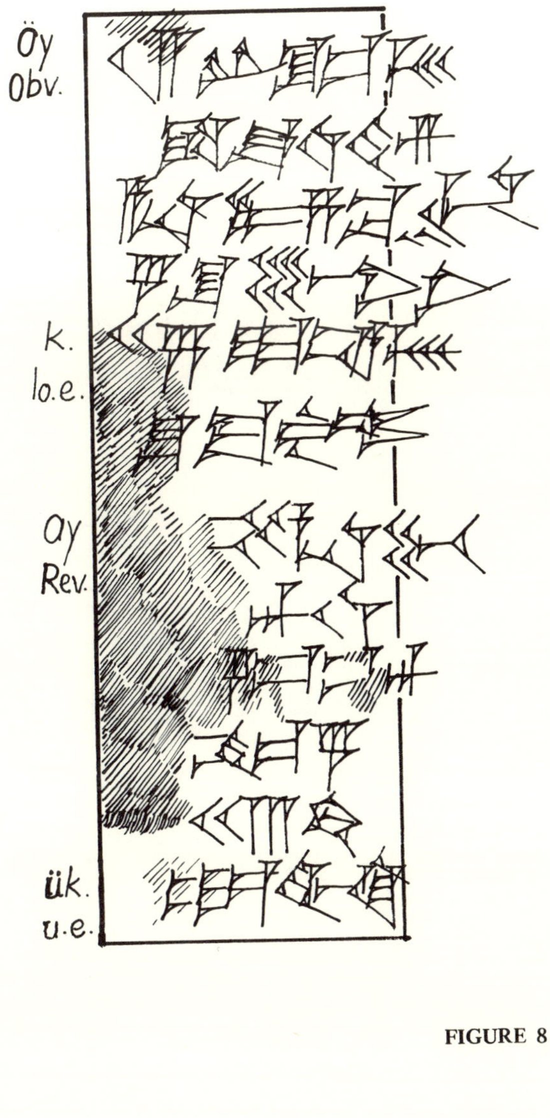

mühür seal
[nu-úr-] ^{d}utu
[dumu ^{d}]utu-ma-an-sum

traces

FIGURE 8

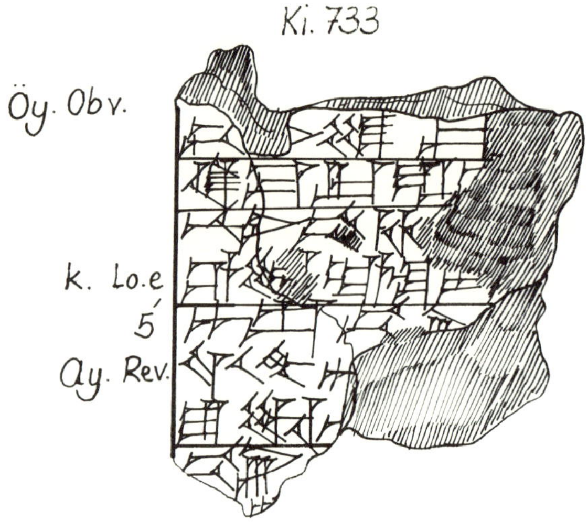
Ki. 733
Öy. Obv.
k. Lo.e
5´
Ay. Rev.

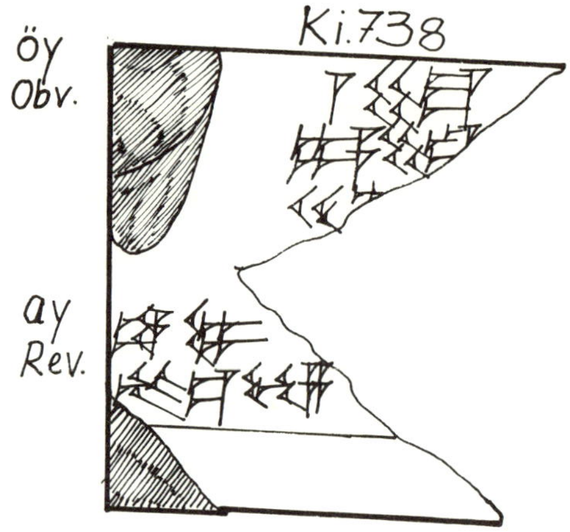
Ki.738
Öy
Obv.
ay
Rev.

Ki.767
Önyüz tamamiyle
bozulmuş
Obv. completely
destroyed

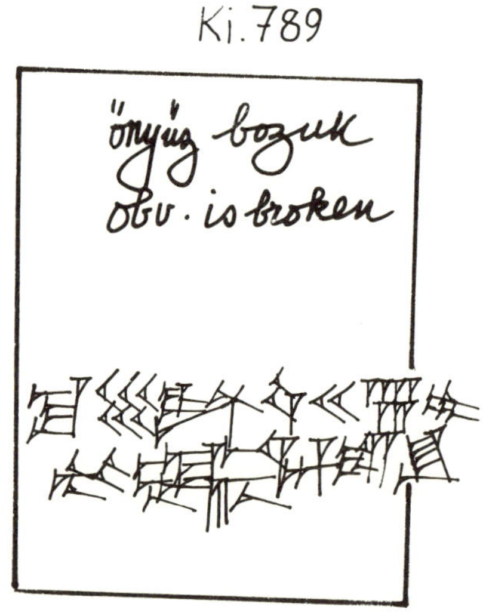
Ki.789
önyüz bozuk
Obv. is broken

FIGURE 9

Ki. 808

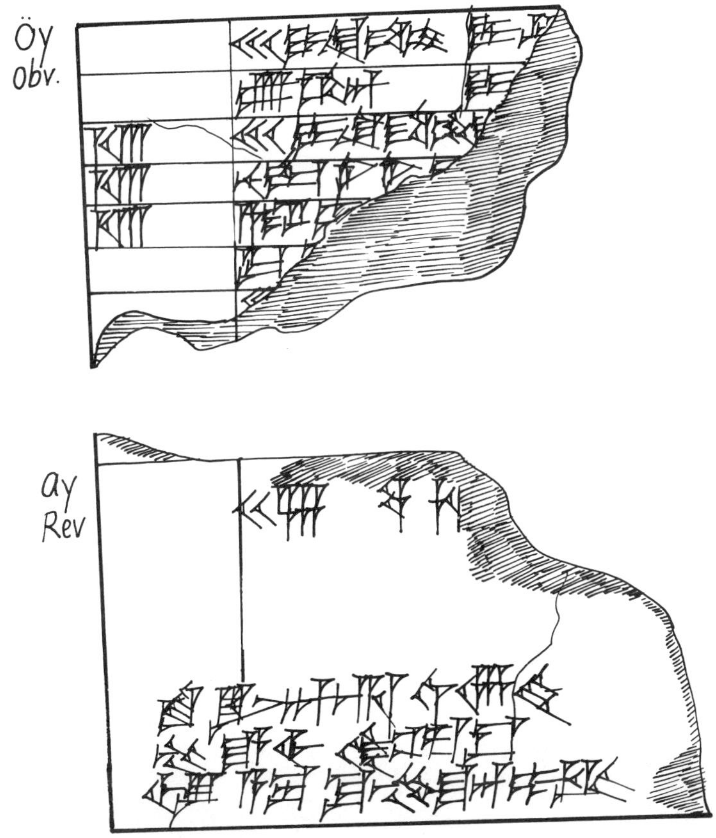

FIGURE 10

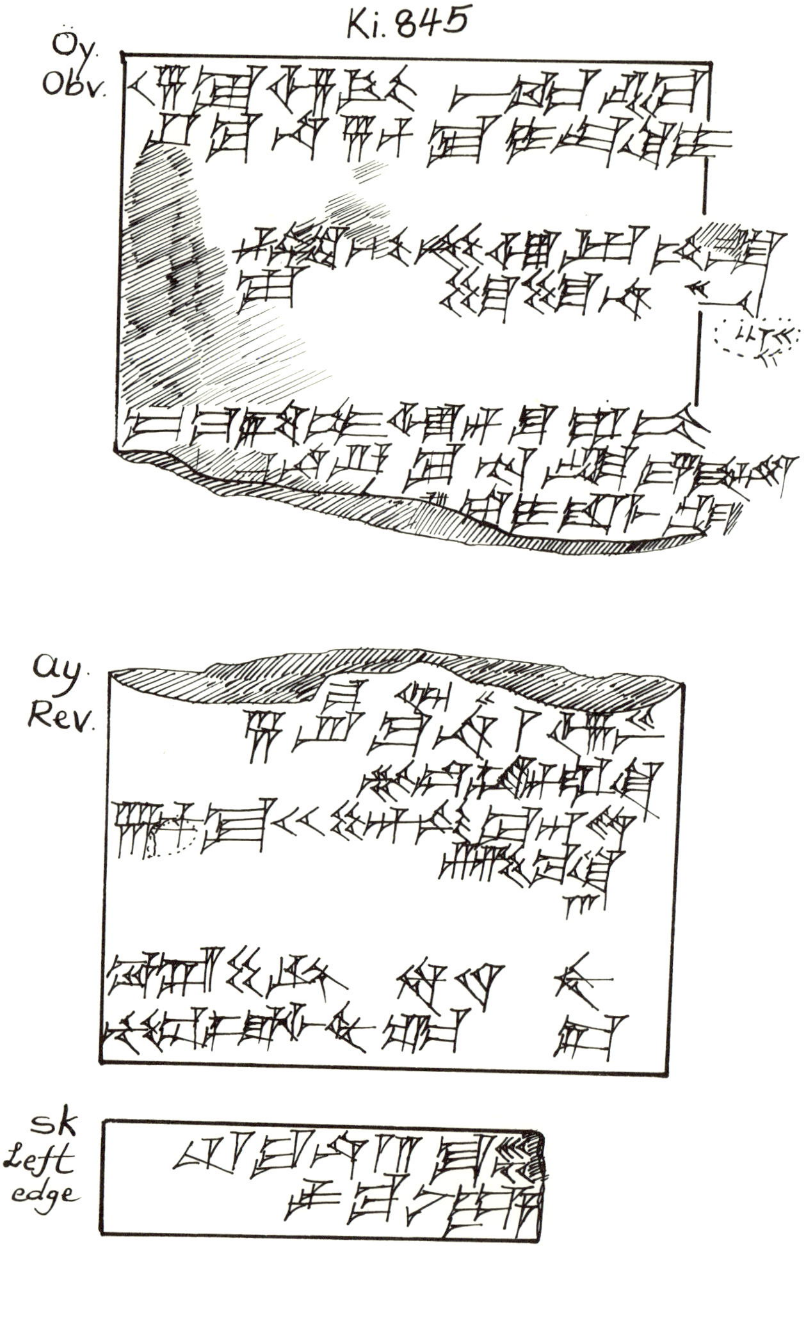

FIGURE 11

Ki.878

Öy.
Obv.

k.
Lo.e.

ay
Rev.

Ki.863

Öy
Obv.

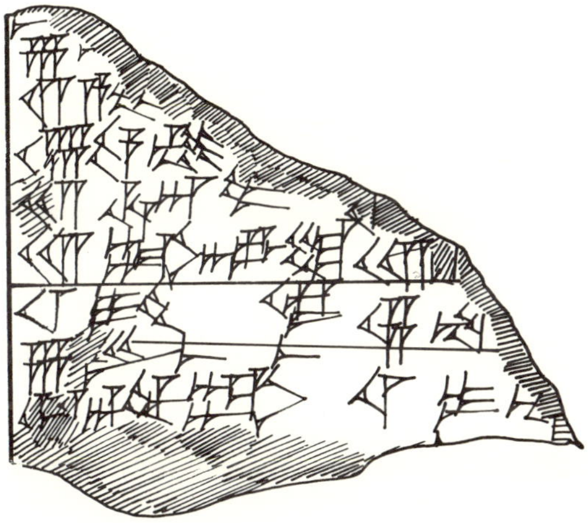

ay
Rev.

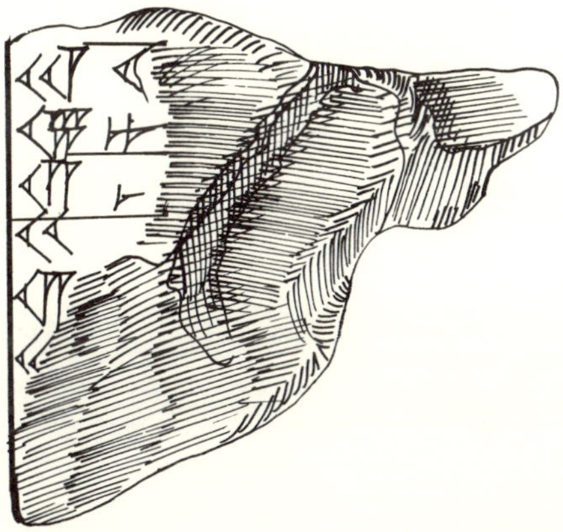

Sk.
left edge

Ki. 883

Öy
Obv.

ay
Rev.

Ük
upper
edge

FIGURE 12

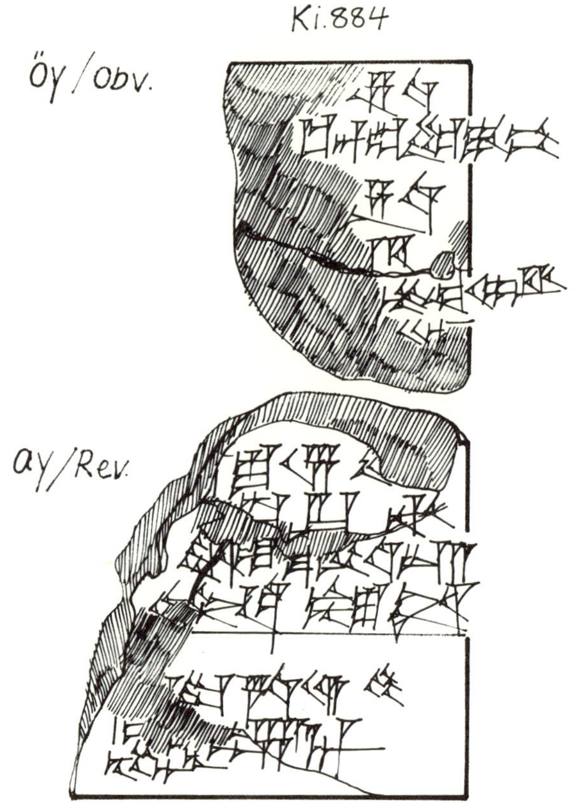

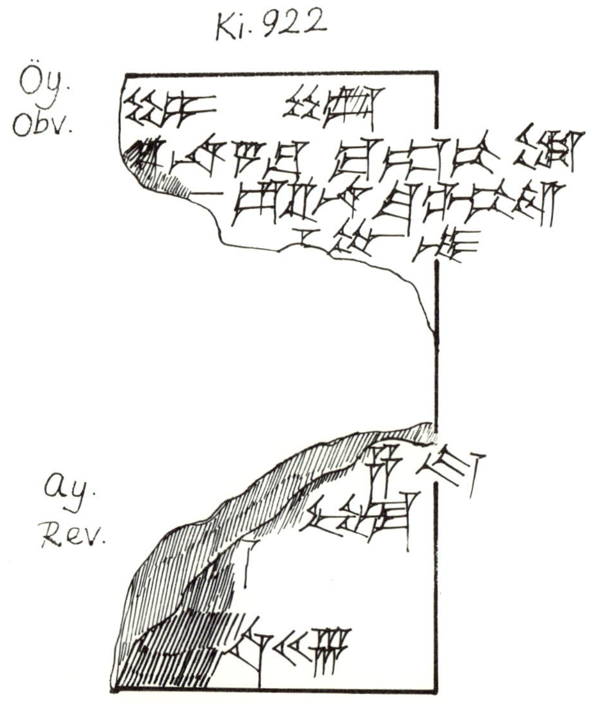

FIGURE 13

Ki. 946

öy
Obv.

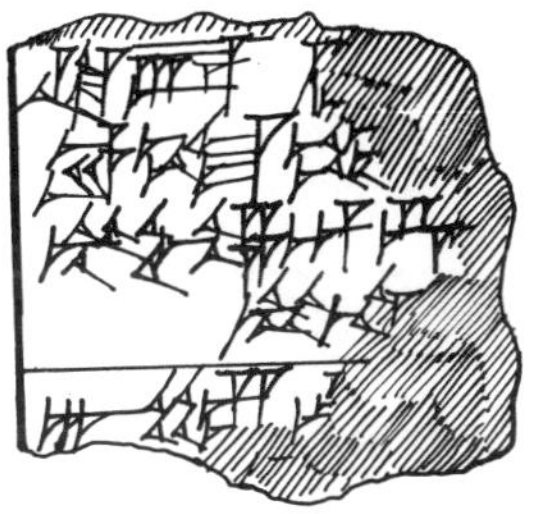

Ki. 960

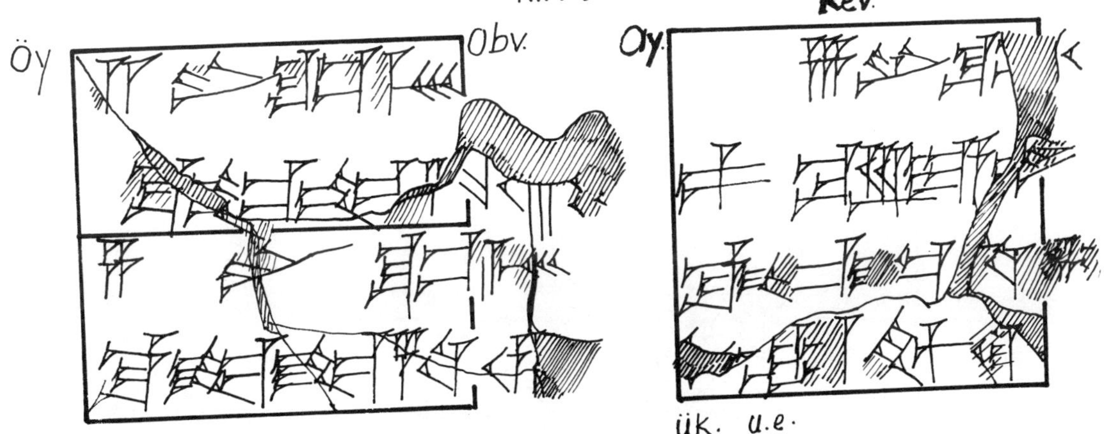

mühür seal

[^{d}AMAR.UD-na-ṣi-]ir
dumu ab-[di]-ìl
ìr-[^{d}na]-bi-um

FIGURE 14

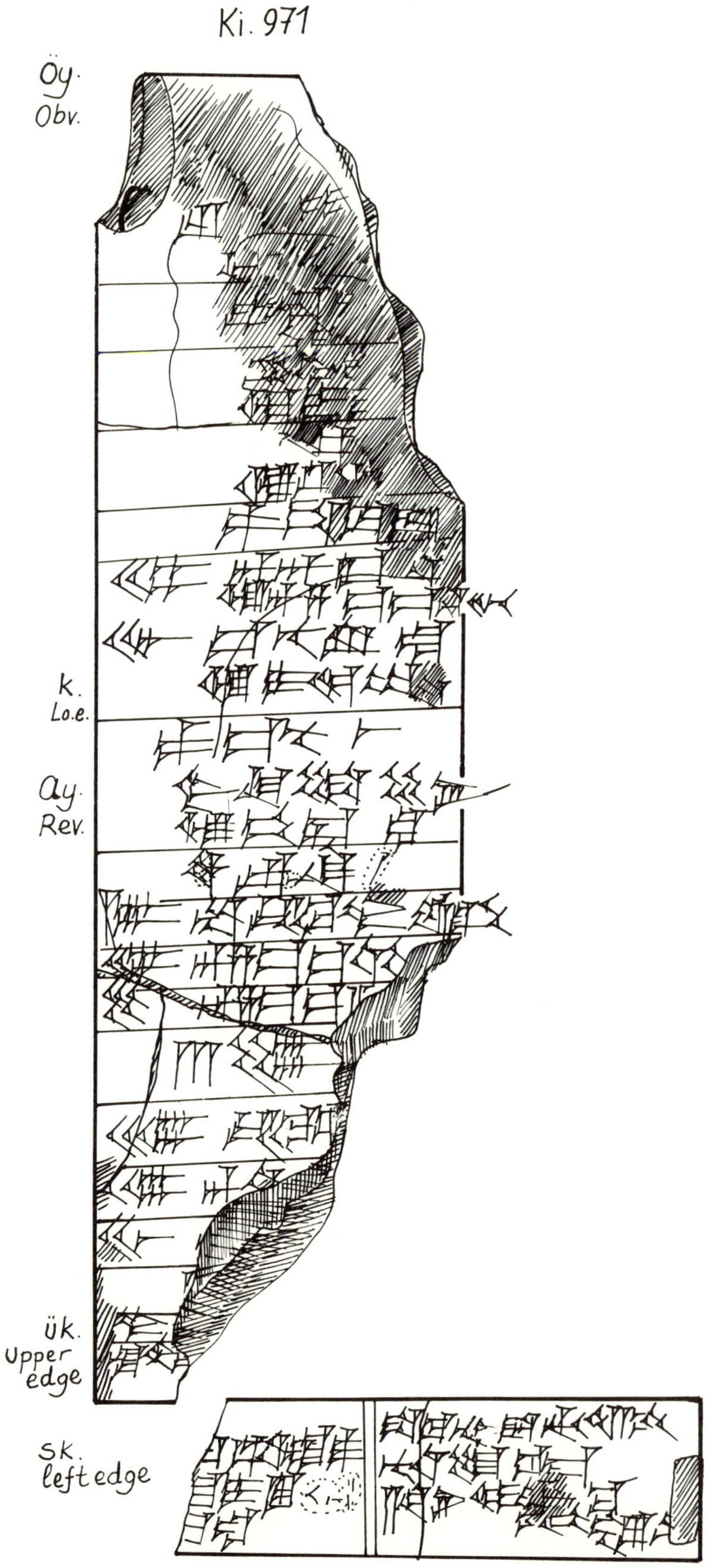

FIGURE 15

Ki.984

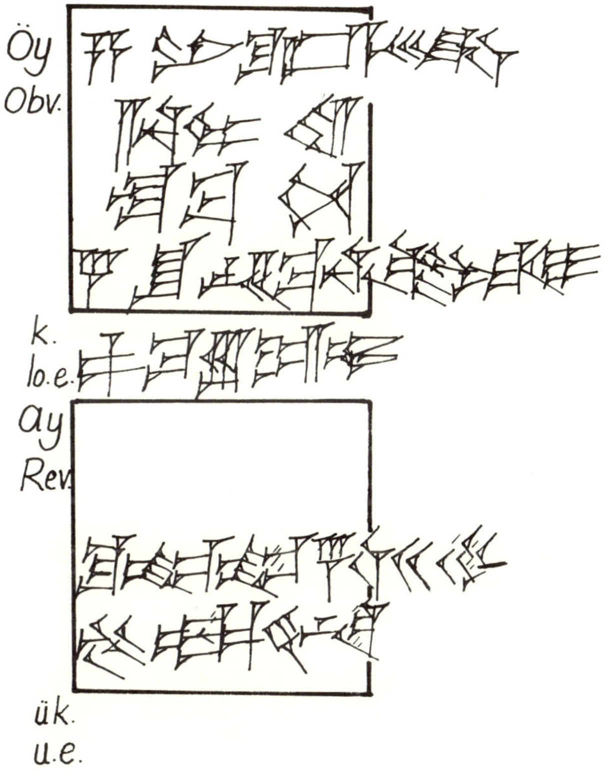

mühür seal
^{d}AMAR·UD-[na-ṣi]-ir
dumu ab-di-ìl
ìr-^{d}na-bi-um

Ki.990

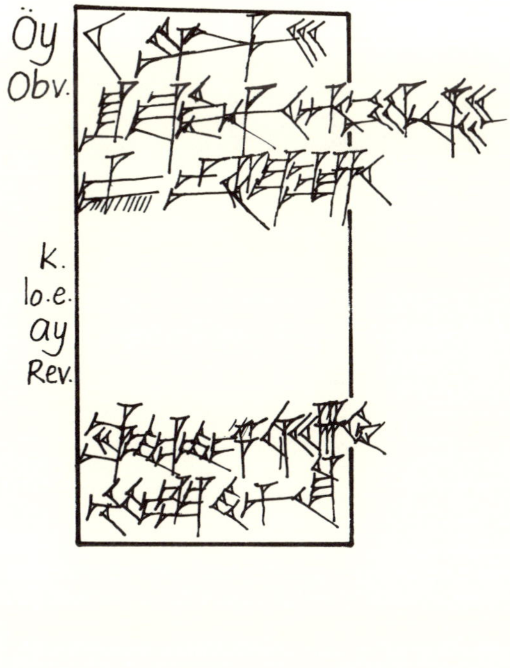

FIGURE 16

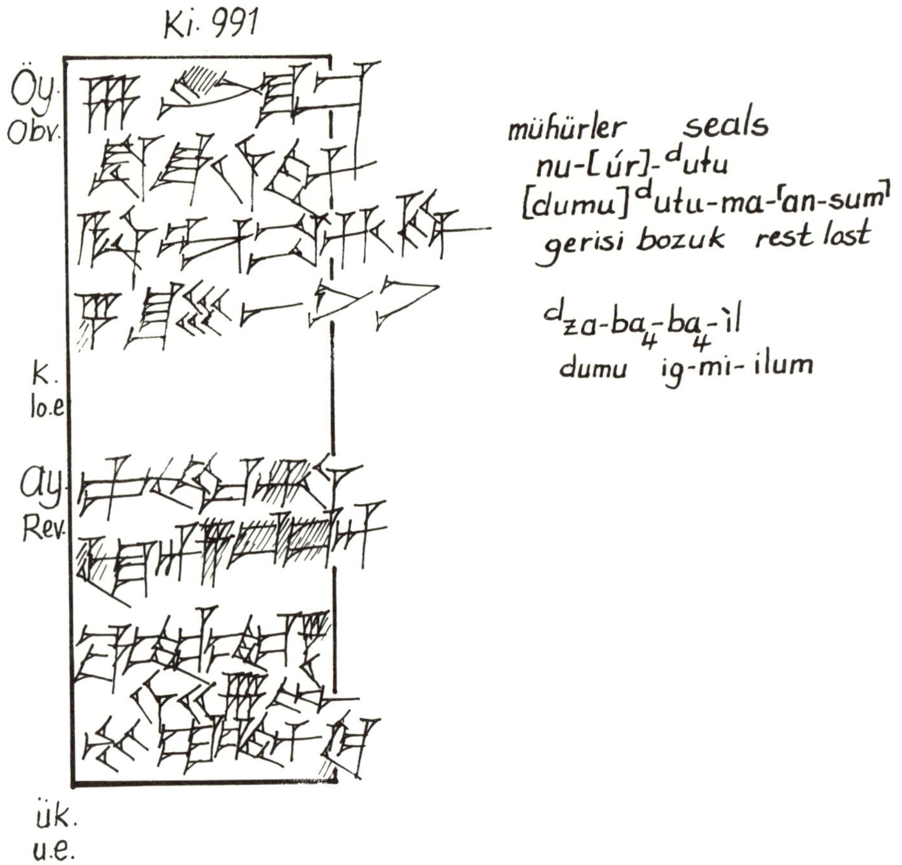
Ki. 991
Öy.
Obv.
K.
lo.e
ay.
Rev.
ük.
u.e.
mühürler seals
nu-[úr]-dutu
[dumu] dutu-ma-⌜an-sum⌝
gerisi bozuk rest lost
dza-ba4-ba4-ìl
dumu ig-mi-ilum

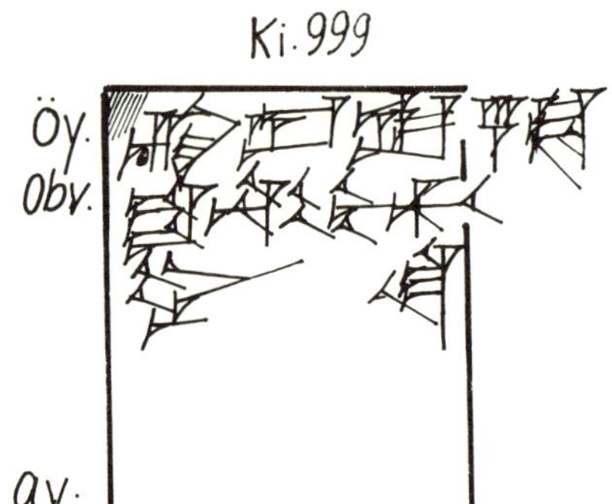
Ki. 999
Öy.
Obv.
ay.
Rev.

FIGURE 17

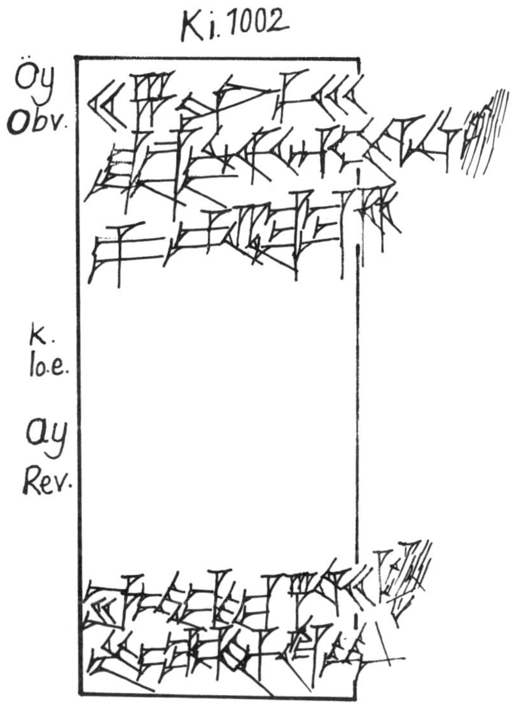

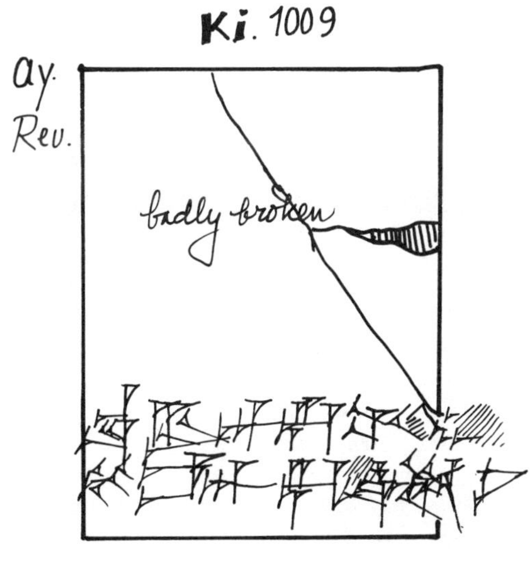

FIGURE 18

Ki. 1017

Öy.
Obv.

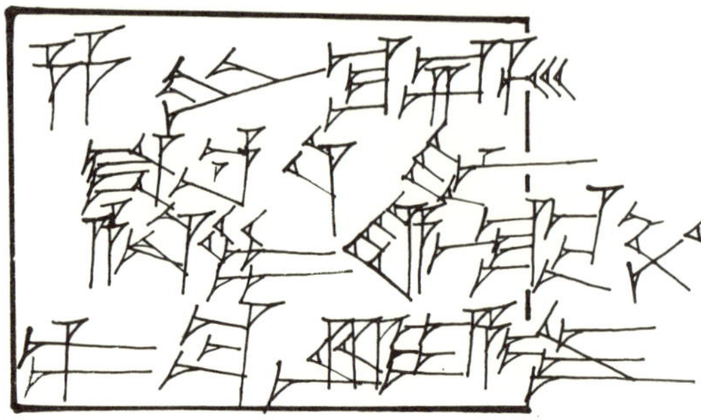

mühür seal

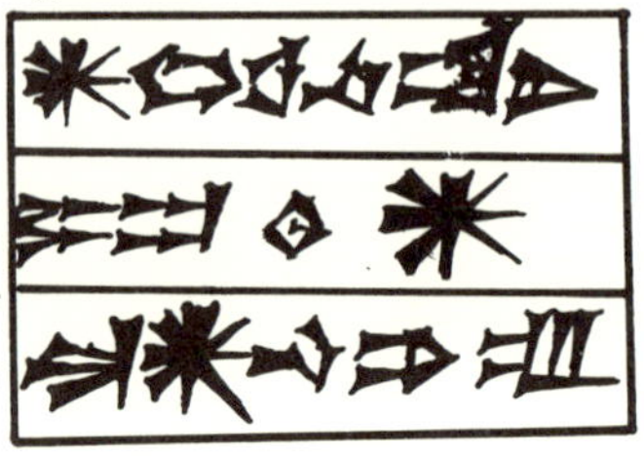

K.
lo.e.

Ay.
Rev.

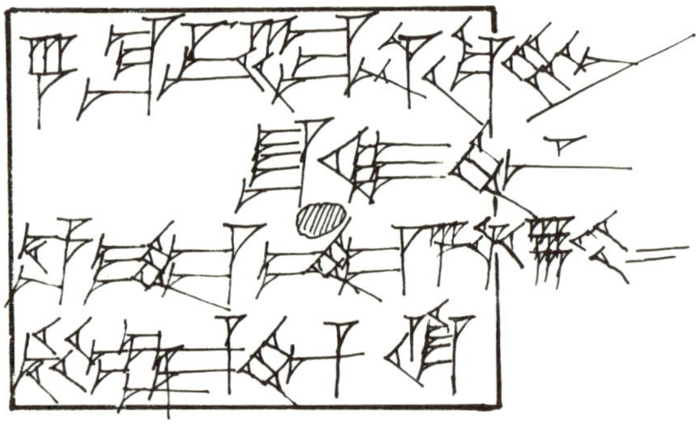

Ük.
u.e.

Ki. 1023

Öy.
Obv.

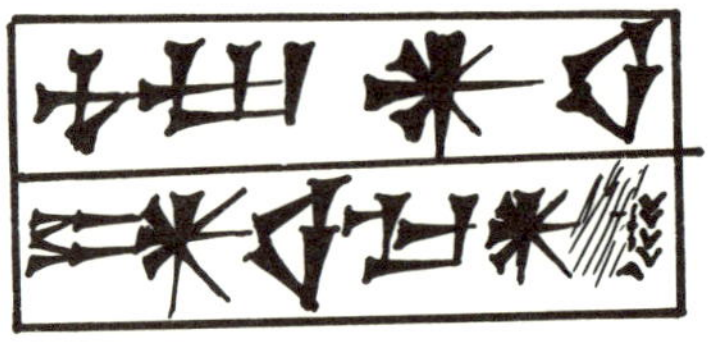

mühür seal
^{d}za-ba$_4$-ba$_4$-il
gerisi bozuk rest lost

K.
lo.e.

Ay.
Rev.

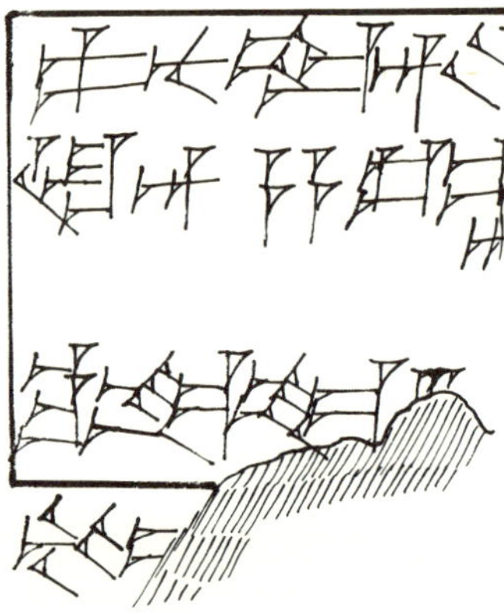

Ük.
u.e.

FIGURE 19

Ki. 1024

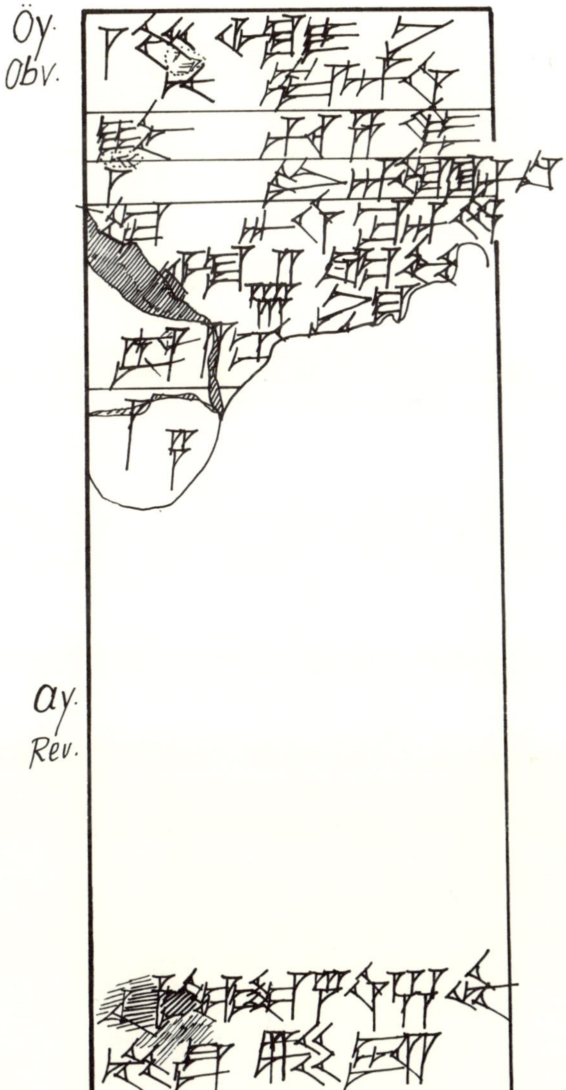

Ki. 1027

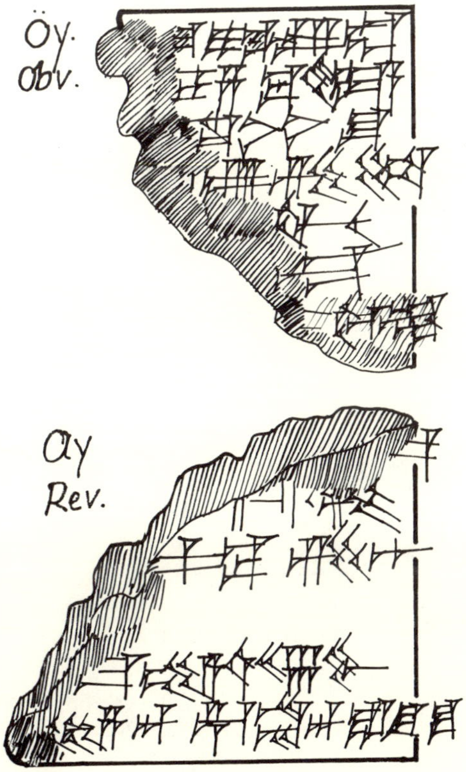

FIGURE 20

Ki. 1034

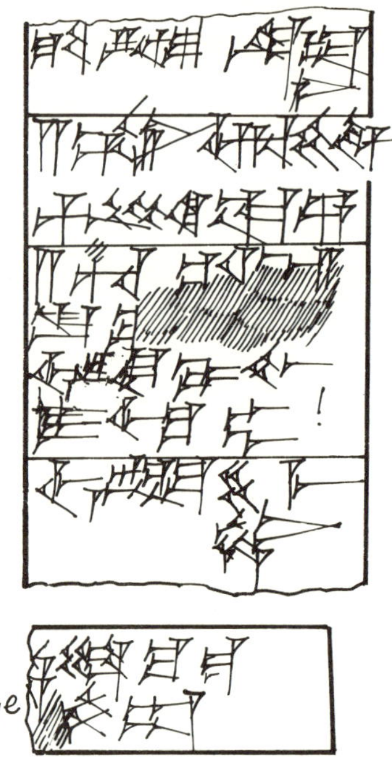

Ki.1036

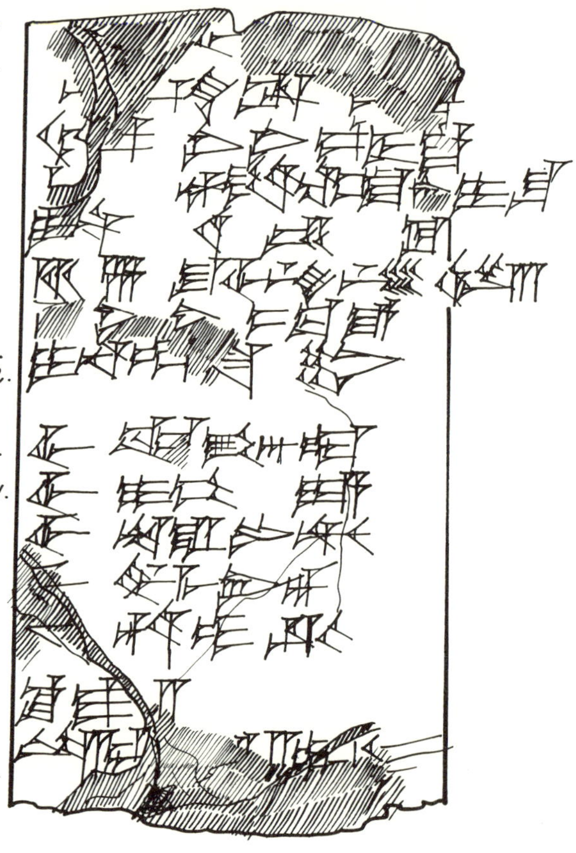

FIGURE 21

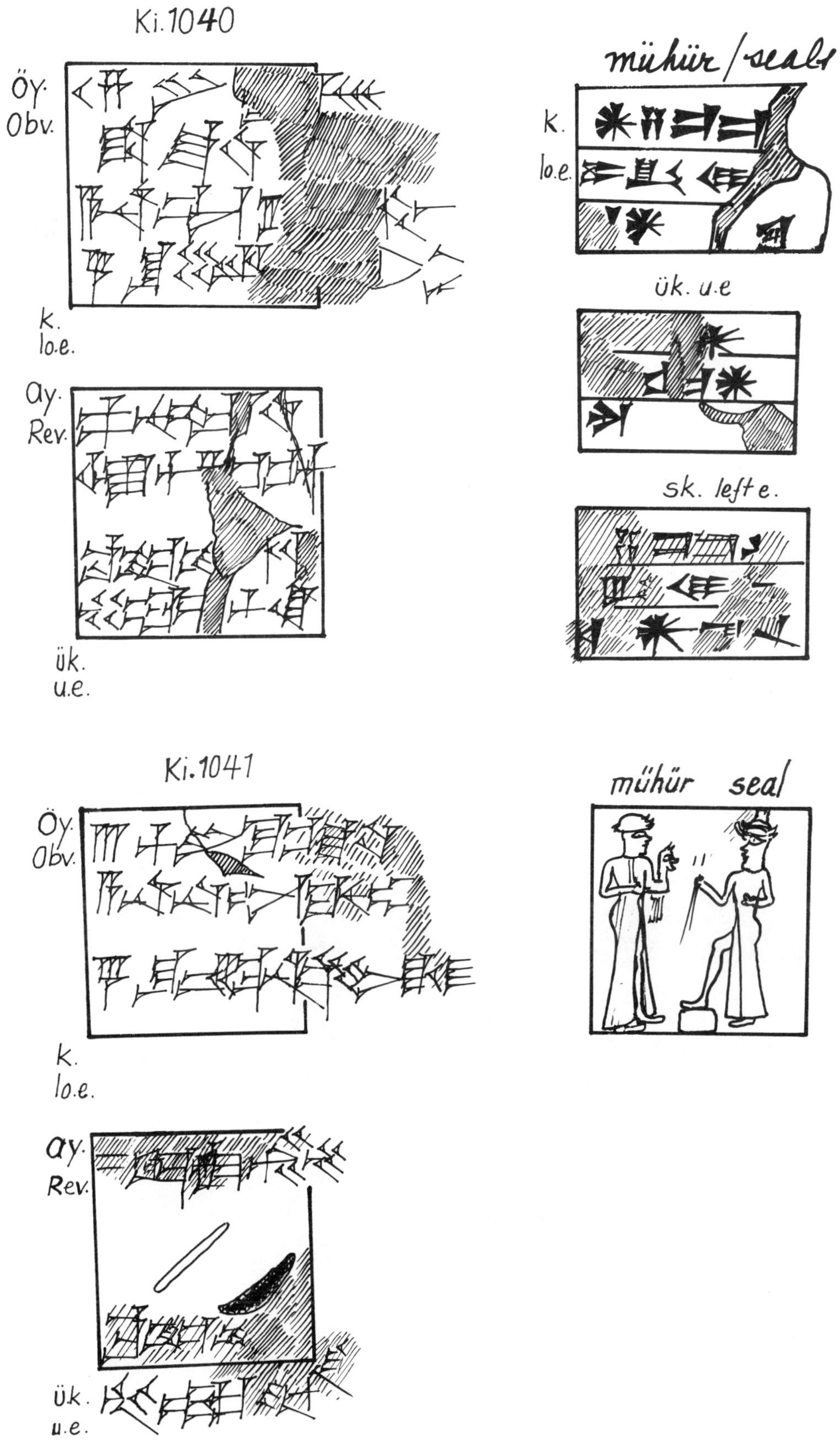
Ki.1040
Öy. Obv.
k. lo.e.
ay. Rev.
ük. u.e.
mühür / seals
k.
lo.e.
ük. u.e
sk. left e.
Ki.1041
Öy. Obv.
k. lo.e.
ay. Rev.
ük. u.e.
mühür seal

FIGURE 22

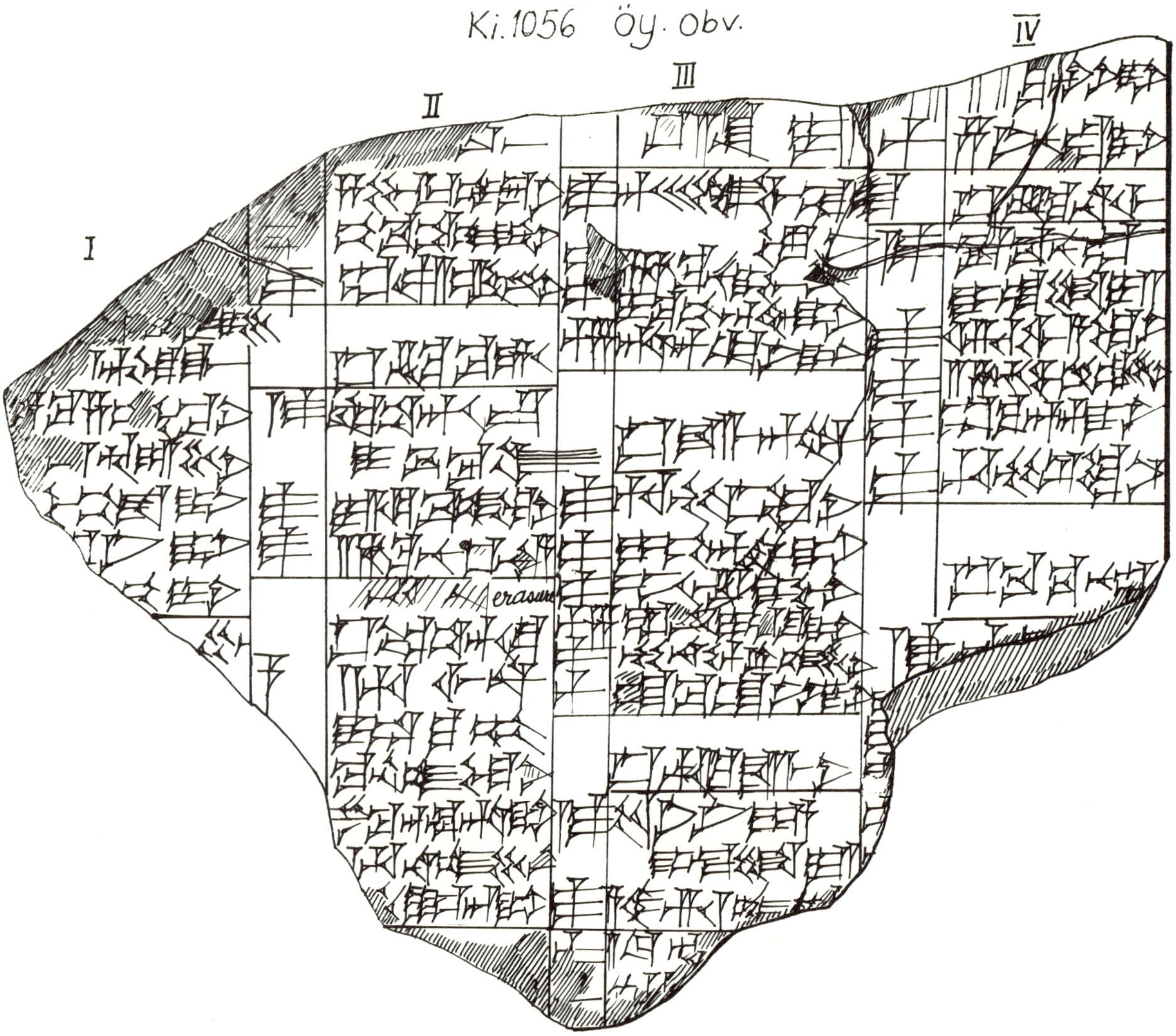

FIGURE 23

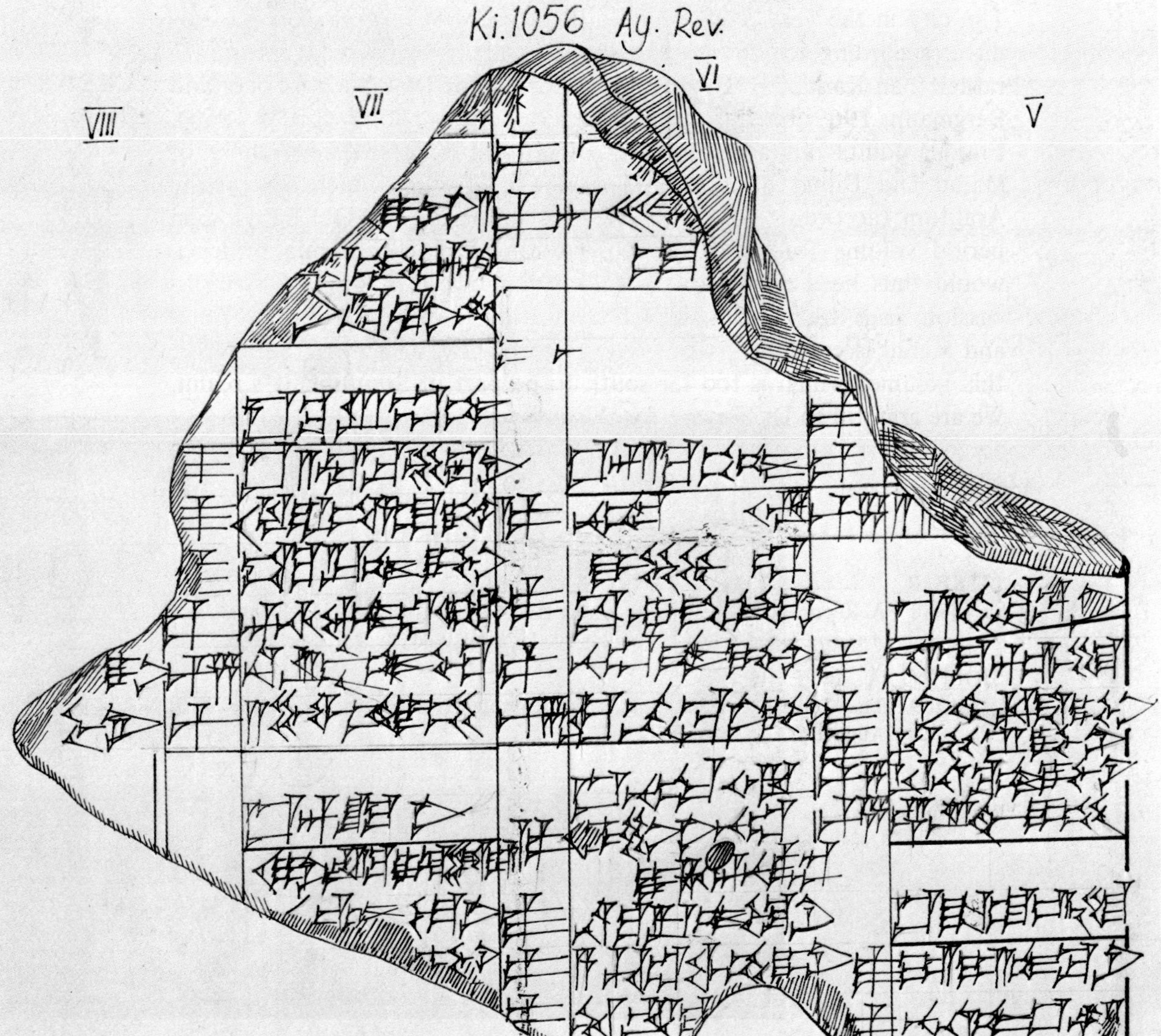

FIGURE 24

Ki 607 obv.

Ki 607 rev.

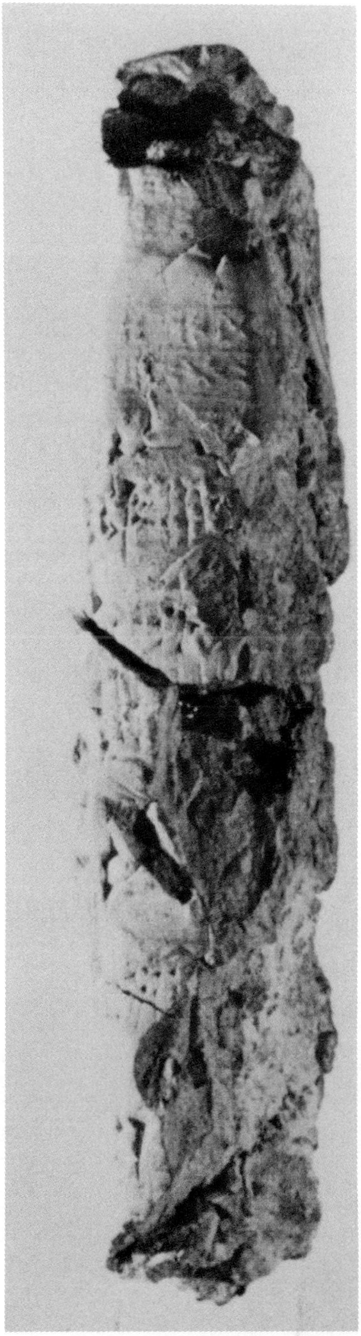

Ki 607 right edge

Ki 607 left edge

Ki 618 envelope

Ki 618 bottom edge

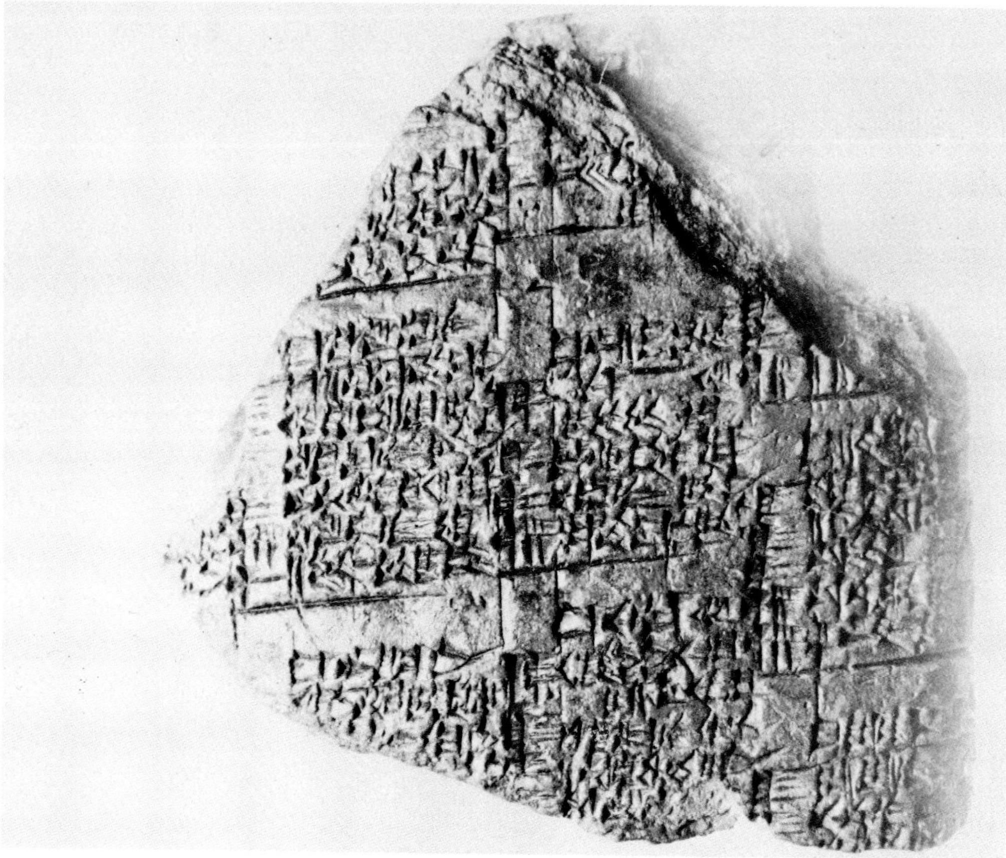

Ki 1056 rev.

Ki 1056 obv.